SYMBOL

A general introductio
symbols and their associations.

SYMBOLISM

The Universal Language

by

J. C. COOPER

Illustrations by G.E. Archer

THE AQUARIAN PRESS
Wellingborough, Northamptonshire

First published 1982
Third Impression 1985

British Library Cataloguing in Publication Data

Cooper, J. C.
  Symbolism.
  1. Symbolism
  I. Title
  302.2   CB475

  ISBN 0-85030-279-X

Printed and bound in Great Britain

Contents

1. Symbols and the Archetypal

Few people realize how totally their everyday lives are imbued with and controlled by symbols, mostly of ancient lineage; symbols that have come down to them not only through the ages but through many different races, cultures and religions. Today, for the average person, a symbol is an empty thing, little more than a sign conveying no other meaning than its outward appearance suggests. For example, a triangle is an accepted sign for danger, whereas the full symbolism of the triangle is both ancient and religious and almost endless in its implications. Signs are concerned with ordinary life; symbols contain an inner archetypal meaning leading to higher realities.

We live in a world of symbols, most of which are either not understood through ignorance or taken so much for granted that their real significance is overlooked. Many we fail to recognize when we meet them. Symbolism is a treasure-house of the past and holds meaning for the present; it has not been invented by individuals but has grown naturally out of the need for expression in a medium that transcends the limitations of words yet speaks a language that can be understood by all, so that from the moment of our birth to the time of our death we use symbols that were current in ancient times and lands. The bride of this age, for instance, wearing wreath, veil, white dress and ring, adopts the same symbols of virginity, fecundity and union that were used by brides who lived, married and died thousands of years ago.

Although most symbols are based on religious concepts and an agricultural way of life, even town-dwellers, industrialists and sceptics, or the merely uninterested, find themselves caught up in them in everyday life. They may have little or no understanding of those symbols, but at the same time they evince a nostalgia for them and for the way of life they are systematically destroying.

The need to understand symbols is great, and never more so than today when so many values are crumbling and nothing is put in their place. Life is full of everything except meaning and as material prosperity has increased, so serenity, peace of mind and happiness have decreased and been replaced by fear, violence, uncertainty and the breakdown of values. Man needs to gain an identity, to search for the answer to the question 'who am I?', to find out what meaning the individual has in the universe, and to pass beyond the material to find the soul.

To understand our symbols is to help to understand ourselves and many of our deep-rooted and instinctive actions and reactions; what our beliefs, superstitions and fears are based on, and why certain beliefs and actions are so persistent and universal. Superstitions are only outworn beliefs, symbols, or once-valid premises from which the life has gone and the true significance been lost, though the form remains. They are the ghosts of former facts and faiths and, like ghosts, remain active long after the real life has departed, haunting the scenes of their former power. For example, we are told as children that Father Christmas comes down the chimney with his gifts and any requests to him must be asked for up the chimney or sent up in the flames. Why? Why can't he come in by the easier door? And what is the chimney other than a convenient way of getting rid of the smoke of the fire? But traditionally and symbolically the chimney was the opening heavenwards and as a hole in the roof it was the Sky Gate, the Sun Door, by which the spirit of man could travel from one world to the other and through which the spirit of heaven could descend. Santa Claus coming down the chimney thus symbolizes gifts brought direct from heaven instead of through the earthly door.

Symbols are an international language; those such as the cross, swastika, circle, tree and serpent, appear in every developed culture as well as in many earlier or more primitive societies; they span the ages from the remote civilizations of the Aryans, Sumerians, Chinese and Egyptians up to the present time. But the symbol is not a static thing, fixed once and for all; it can grow and expand, include other meanings and become ambivalent, meaning one thing in one culture and age but having a different connotation in another. Thus the serpent, universally a symbol of wisdom, can in the West depict evil and the devil; but, in the East, where it appears as the dragon, it stands for supreme spiritual power. Its changing skin universally represents renewal and rebirth, while, on the other hand, the snake can symbolize poison and death. Symbols, as Mircea Eliade says, help to make man one with the rhythms of nature, integrating him into a larger unity, society and the universe. This is why symbols can have so many levels of meaning; they fit into the infinite variety of nature and man's place in the cosmos.

Although the chief function of symbolism is to reveal an inner meaning, like all religions, it can operate on both the exoteric and esoteric levels; it can be used to conceal as well as to reveal, and in this respect it has always played an important part in secret societies and the occult aspects of initiation ceremonies. The use of symbols was essential in leading the initiate from the limited regions of the rational mind and the world of the senses to that which exists beyond them, the unlimited, infinite 'super'-natural world.

Language itself is symbolic in origin, which explains why poetry preceded prose in expressing thoughts and emotions. Poetry is primarily concerned with man's place in the universe, his reactions to it and the sense of wonder inspired; that is Wordsworth's 'sense of something far more deeply interfused', or Browning's intuition of man's function as mediator:

> Man, once descried, imprints forever
> His presence on all lifeless things: the winds
> Are henceforth voices, wailing or a shout,
> A querulous mutter or a quick gay laugh,
> Never a senseless gust now man is born . . .
> And this to fill us with regard for man,
> With apprehension of his passing worth,
> Desire to work his proper nature out,
> And ascertain his rank and final place.

In spite of the fact that symbols and archetypes are usually spoken of together, they are not identical. The archetype ('arche', means an origin, a cause or beginning, a primordial source, and 'type' implies a copy, imprint or form, usually abstract) but is made manifest by symbols, which bring the abstract (the Platonic Idea) into concrete form as an image, an image which can be shown forth or made in different forms or modes. Dionysius the Areopagite gives an explanation: 'God is the archetypal light. That the seal is not entire and the same in all its impressions . . . is not due to the seal itself but the difference of the substances which share it makes the impression of the one, entire, identical archetype to be different.' The symbol, being derived from the archetype, must lead back to it and merge the finite mind with the infinite.

2. The Centre

There are two ways of looking at the world: the rationalistic, which deals with facts that increase for evermore and tend towards fragmentation and dissipation, or the central, in which man strives after a spiritual centre which is at one and the same time the centre of himself, the world, and of all things. Man instinctively feels himself to be the centre of his world, but, as Mircea Eliade says, we must not envisage this centre in any geometrical sense; it belongs to experience, so there are unlimited centres, many of them even called the 'Centre of the World'. These are found in all great traditions and symbolize 'sacred space', which is a cosmic centre, a place of renewal and immortality. The spiritual quest in life has always been the finding of this sacred centre within. First, like all the great heroes of the quest – Ulysses, Parsifal, the Seekers of the Grail – one journeys outwards towards the circumference, the realm of manifestation, of increasing fragmentation. From the circumference only a limited view can be obtained, so that any view from that point, being partial, is also in a sense false. After endless difficulties, trials and adventures, in which the Seeker is usually helped by guides of various sorts, the point comes when it is realized that Truth, the Kingdom of Heaven, is within and the journey back to the centre begins. It is, to quote T. S. Eliot, necessary to go a long way through many difficulties to find a place one has never really left. The centre is the point from which all may be viewed in its entirety, the Whole. To be 'off centre' implies error, disharmony and disorder. The centre is also the meeting point at which any state may be changed.

The symbolism of the centre is closely associated with that of the labyrinth, an extremely old and wide-spread formation, the most celebrated being that of the Minotaur at Knossus. Theseus, a hero-saviour, travels the path from the circumference to the centre guided by the golden thread given him by the beautiful Ariadne. Here Theseus is the male adventurer, helped by the powers of feminine intuition and wisdom, the two in co-operation bringing about the death of the savage, sub-human nature. In psychological terms, Ariadne represents the soul, or psyche, which provides the golden thread that brings man back safely from the encounter with the Beast, the dark forces of nature.

The return to the centre is a symbol of Paradise Regained, of attaining and re-establishing the original perfection enjoyed before the Fall, a state in which gods, men and animals lived in perfect accord and spoke the same language. But, again, the centre is difficult to attain and there are trials and dangers on the way. There are labyrinths in places which have been the scene of ancient rites and they also appear in churches and cathedrals such as Chartres, where it is suggested that they were 'walked' as a form of pilgrimage for those who were unable to undertake the long journeys to holy places. They also represent the perplexities and difficulties that confront mankind in the journey through this world, during which the way must be threaded both by individual effort and the help of the divine thread of wisdom. One takes many blind paths and makes many mistakes until that divine, guiding knowledge is found and used.

The Thread of Life
The thread is also the thread of life, of human fate; it binds man to destiny but at the same time provides communication with the divine. The Greeks called it the Golden Thread of Zeus, a golden chain which was the link between heaven and earth. The symbol of the thread is inevitably connected with weaving, the web of life being woven by the divine powers. The earliest representation of this was the Great Mother Goddess weaving the loom of life and destiny. She was often depicted as the Cosmic Spider, or Creator, who spins the thread from its own essence and binds everything to itself. The spider at the centre of the web depicts a world centre and the web is the cosmic plan. The web is also associated with the labyrinth as the dangerous journey to attain the centre. Neither the spinner nor the spun, the Creator nor the created, can ever be separated; they are forever bound by the past, present and future, a process which does not end with physical 'death' but which carries on, through the workings of *karma*, through successive lives. There is, however, a paradox here in the symbolism of

binding, for the deities of binding are also those of loosing and in *yoga*, which means a 'yoke and binding', and religion, which means to 're-bind' are found the means of gaining complete freedom in attaining the centre and finding the release of realization or enlightenment.

In temples and churches the altar is the sacred centre, both in time and space, while every sacred building represents a spiritual world centre, a meeting place for all three worlds, being in contact with the earth, the heavens and the underworld. The domes of temples and spires of churches symbolize aspiration heavenwards, the vertical bond between earth and heaven, God and man. The main body of the building lies horizontal on the plane of human experience and existence, while the crypt, or the cave-temple, represents the dark womb, death and rebirth.

The Hearth

In the home, the hearth has always symbolized an interior spiritual centre. The returning home of all wanderers, pilgrims and questers is the journey back to hearth and home. The hearth was, traditionally, at the centre; in early Greek houses the hearth was circular and literally at the centre of the dwelling, with the smoke going out at the apex, as it still does in nomadic tents. In Hinduism, the Vedic round hearth represents the earth, the dwelling of man, with the fire as the realm of the gods and the spirit, though this symbolism of the hearth as the place of the spirit of fire is universal. We see this central position of the hearth in the Latin word *focus* and the French *foyer*, the hearth being the focal point of rites in the home. Keary says, in his *Dawn of History*: 'The hearth was in the midst of the dwelling; that hearth was to each member of the household, as it were, an *umbillicus orbis*, a navel of the earth … "hearth" being only another form of "earth", as in the German "erde" or "herde". The hearth was where the whole family assembled and shared food and warmth and where the guest was given the place of honour.'

The fault of modern architecture is that it has lost this essential symbolism and so builds empty shells, without a spirit in the body, and it is one of the evils of television that it destroys the focal point of the hearth, with all its family associations, communication and consolidation, and disperses the attention outwards to the outer, profane world, so breaking the once sacred family unity and bringing alien influences into the home. Blocks of flats have the same adverse effect in that they have no hearth-centre and suspend their dwellers in mid-air, out of touch with the earth and with no outlet heavenwards; a total divorce from man's natural environment.

The chimney of the house, or the round hole at the top of the tent, with smoke rising upwards through it, gives direct communication with the realm above and depicts man's aspiration and ability to be in touch with both worlds. Smoke is a symbol of prayer ascending, both from the sacred hearth in the home and from the altars of temples and churches in incense. It was also an invitation to the deity to descend; the column of smoke is equated with a world axis by means of which a two-way communication is possible. The earth of the hearth is associated with the feminine-earth aspect and with the female domination of the home, but the fire is a masculine power, so the two together combine to form the living centre of the house. In many traditions, and notably in Celtic lands, this hearth symbolism went further and the hearth-stone covered the earth which gave access to the underworld and made communication with it and with the dead possible, so that it was a point of contact between all three worlds. Bones found under the hearth in old houses either represented a ritual sacrifice or protection against underworld malefic powers.

The Threshold

To enter the house the threshold must be crossed; this is the passage from the profane outer world into the sacred inner space where no one may enter uninvited. Crossing another person's threshold is entering another world, one in which you are a stranger and so, in certain circumstances, could be at peril. This explains why myths and legends of entering dark forests, sinking in water, passing through a door in a wall, or going through a looking glass, are all threshold symbols of entering unknown and perilous states, finding oneself in a strange place where anything can happen.

Because this meeting place of the natural and supernatural powers is dangerous, it is bad luck to touch it; so the threshold is always stepped over and the bride is protected by being carried over it by the bridegroom, who, at the wedding, assumes responsibility for her welfare and sets her down safely in the new world they will share together. Sometimes iron was placed under the threshold to prevent any evil or supernatural powers entering, such as witches, elves or fairies, who are all well known to be afraid of any form of iron. This, too, is the reason for horseshoes being nailed over the doors of houses, stables or byres where the people or animals within need protection from dangerous forces without. The horseshoe is not only iron but also a protective symbol. It represents the horns of the crescent moon of the Great Mother Goddess. Horns have always depicted power and protection, while the horse, as we shall see, is a highly symbolic animal.

Thresholds of especially sacred places, such as temples or places where treasure was hidden, were guarded by fierce monsters, dragons, serpents, lions and dogs, kept there to scare away enemies or adverse influences. They had, at the same time, another purpose since they signified the difficulties to be overcome before the sacred realm could be entered or the spiritual treasure or the centre attained. They also scared away the unworthy and the half-hearted and those unwilling to risk all in the quest for the centre and wisdom.

The door, too, is associated with the passage from one state to another, the entrance to a new life, and the coming under the protective and sheltering aspect of the feminine power. But the door has the added significance of hope, of opening out, of opportunity – a symbolism shared by the window, which is not only opening and opportunity but an expansion of view and possibilities of awareness.

Obviously stairs are equated with ascension and so indicate the possibility of moving from one state of consciousness to another and of transcendence. Any climbing denotes ascent heavenwards. Spiral staircases depict the sun's movement, winding stairs symbolize the mysterious, the unknown, the future, while the steps of stairs or ladders represent the ability to ascend to higher planes and in this connection they are associated with the steps of initiation. Passing up and down ladders, as with Jacob's ladder, depicts the two-way traffic between earthly and heavenly powers. Before the Fall there was a ladder between heaven and earth so that there could be constant communion between God and man; but at the loss of Paradise, this communication was broken, the ladder was lost, and can now only be found again through initiation or the quest for Paradise Regained, the return to the Centre.

Since the house stands for the enclosing, protecting feminine power, to go into it is to enter the female domain, which is not only protective but also provides nourishment in food and warmth in clothing. The provision of these is the woman's concern, typifying the Mother, the Great Nourisher, Mother Earth.

Bread and Salt

In the provision of food, bread and salt are two of the most basic necessities and, together, they symbolize welcome, hospitality and good faith. To break bread with anyone, to eat salt in a house, a giving and accepting of hospitality, immediately imposes an obligation on both giver and receiver; it binds them together in friendship and should exclude any possibility of either harming the other. The wayfarer, entering a strange house, not only comes in out of the cold (or the heat, as the case might be), but from the possibility of hostile and dangerous forces in the world without. He entered into the shelter of the home and felt doubly safe once he had been offered bread and salt. Salt is that which is incorruptible and so is associated with permanence and, by extension, immortality. It also stands for wisdom, the supremely worthwhile, the 'salt of the earth'. (If someone is worthless, they are said to be 'not worth their salt'.) Later on salt was associated with piquance, since any food without salt tastes flat and uninteresting, and hence with wit, its pungency is expressed by having 'a salted tongue'. Not only was salt a symbol of immortality but also of truth. In such widely differing cultures as the Norse and the Roman, salt was placed on the tongue of an infant and was used in holy water at some ceremonies of baptism or consecration, while during funeral rites, it protected the dead from evil spirits.

Bread is also a symbol of life. It is the food of the physical body, but when it is blest and consecrated in religious rites it becomes the food of the soul. Eating anything has, from time immemorial, been regarded as partaking of and absorbing the quality of the thing eaten. The most elementary example of this is cannibalism, when the flesh of the enemy is eaten. This not only triumphs over the slain enemy but also transmits his powers by absorbing them into the system. With the same idea in mind, fish, which are prolific breeders and a symbol of fecundity, were eaten to induce fertility. Fish was always eaten at the feasts of the Mother Goddess, especially under her guise of Artemis/Atargatis (whose son Ichthys was the sacred fish), Isis and Venus. The Mother is also the Moon Goddess, Queen of Heaven. She controls the waters and her day is Friday, so that fish was eaten in her honour on that day. The priests of Atargatis had special sacred fish ponds and fish was their eucharistic food.

The Egg

The egg is a universal symbol of creation and life and hence of resurrection. In initiation it can symbolize the 'twice born', its laying being one birth and its hatching the second. That the world began with the Cosmic Egg is both an ancient and universal idea. Symbolically, it can be represented by the sphere, the Great Round; it is the beginning of all things, and the hidden mystery of existence, containing the universe and all possibilities. In it all opposites are contained but unified. This is perfectly expressed in the well-known Chinese *yin-yang* symbol.

In Hindu and Egyptian traditions, the egg as the source of all creation is particularly notable. In the former, the divine bird laid the golden cosmic egg on the primordial waters. From it sprang Brahma and the two halves formed heaven and earth. The cosmic tree is sometimes depicted as growing from the golden egg floating on the waters of chaos. In the Egyptian tradition, the Nile Goose laid the cosmic egg from which Ra, the Sun, was hatched. The two halves of the hatched egg also appear in Greek myth, where they are worn as domed caps by the Dioscuri, born of the egg laid by Leda, who was fertilized by Zeus in the form of a swan. In China the yolk was the sky and the albumen the earth.

The Alchemist's egg

The egg is also closely associated with the serpent. An alternative Egyptian allegory was that Kneph, the Serpent, produced the cosmic egg from his mouth, symbolizing the Logos. Orphism, holding the egg to be the mystery of life, of creation and resurrection, often depicted it as surrounded by Ouroboros, the circular serpent holding its tail in its mouth, a figure which in itself also symbolizes potentiality, totality and primordial unity. The Druids called the cosmic egg the 'Egg of the Serpent'. In Alchemy the white flower, silver, the feminine, and the red flower, gold, the masculine, are both contained in and grow out of the egg, and the philosophers' egg is the symbol of creation. As will be seen later, the egg of creation and resurrection is closely associated with the Spring Festival of new life at Easter.

3. The Circle

Roundness is the most natural and perfect shape in nature. Not surprisingly, the circle has always and universally been held as a sacred symbol, one which expresses archetypal wholeness and totality and therefore divinity. Hermes Trismegistus said: 'God is a circle whose centre is everywhere and circumference nowhere.' In a modern context, when Christian missionaries asked the Red Indians about their God they drew the circle of the Feathered Sun, a symbol which the limited view of the missionaries was unable to appreciate but which, in fact, is a perfect metaphysical ideograph with its red 'feathers' pointing inwards and the black outwards, depicting the two-way movement of power – inwards towards the centre and outwards to the circumference, containing everything within itself.

With the cross, the circle is one of the most complex of symbols. Having no end, it obviously stands for eternity and spacelessness since it has no above or below. It represents the annulment of both time and space, but as the round, the wheel, it also signifies perpetual recurrence and cyclic movement.

The symbols of the circle and the centre are not only universal but pre-historical, and are depicted on the earliest objects and artifacts. They later developed to the highest degree in the mandala, which combines the three most significant symbols, the circle, the square or cross, and the centre, which in the mandala can be a figure, a lotus, a flame, or some point for concentration. The word comes from the Arabic *Al mandal*, the circle; it is 'the systematic arrangement of symbols on which the process of visualization is based'. In Tibetan Buddhism, where it plays a highly important part, it means both the centre and that which surrounds it, hence a world image into which the meditator must penetrate, imagining him- or herself as the centre of the mandala and entering into Buddahood. It represents the whole cosmic drama and, like the labyrinth, also stands for the pilgrimage of the soul through the world. The centre, when reached, is also the Sky Door and the means of reaching the heavens. The centre of the circle is always a place of power, since it is an enclosed space, safe from hostile forces. This symbolism of the circle is carried from the highest to the lowest, from the sacred centre of the mandalaand the *chakra*, the spiritual centre represented by the lotus or the wheel, to the 'magic circle' of the magician, sorcerer or witch.

The Hindu temple is constructed in the form of a mandala. This is seen particularly clearly at Borobadur, where the whole universe is represented in the various terraces or 'levels', as the planes or heavens, the whole being built as a cosmic mountain, symbol of the centre of the world. There are gates and doors at the four cardinal points, bringing in the square, and the whole encloses Time and Space. Demons sometimes depicted in the mandala or on the walls of temples symbolize the dangerous and menacing aspects of the psychic powers and forces of passion and desire which threaten and impede progress towards the light.

Defensive positions are also built on the pattern of the circle and square, with the innermost centre as the sacred, focal point. Romulus, when building Rome, set up an altar at the centre and built ramparts round as a trench. Plutarch says that the name of 'world' – *mundes* – was given to that trench 'as to the universe itself'. This symbolism of the sacred centre of the circle is the repetition of an archetype. As Mircea Eliade says: 'Man constantly feels the need to "realize" archetypes, even down to the lowest level of his immediate existence; it is a longing for transcendent forms – in this instance for sacred space.' We see, for example, the perpetuation of this symbolism at its lowest level in our town centres, regarded as the hub of the society; or we speak of the church or the school being the 'centre' of the village community and all activities 'revolving' round it. The circle is also the form of the encampment of the tents of nomads, whether those of Europe, Asia or North America. On another plane, the circle symbolizes dynamic movement as opposed to the static square of the houses and plots of land of city dwellers and agriculturalists. But wherever it occurs, it is a symbol of sacred space, of wholeness and divinity.

The revolving of the circle naturally brings in the symbolism of the wheel and the sun. The sun is always round and revolving in the heavens, while the moon changes shape and regularly disappears. The moon, associated with the waters and all that is moving and rhythmic, is, with a few exceptions, the symbol of the feminine powers in the universe, the Mother Goddess, while the sun is the masculine power, the great symbol of the Sky God. The turning of the wheel also depicts the inexorable and relentless movement of Time and Fate. In Hinduism and Buddhism, this is used as a particularly evocative symbol in which the circumference of the wheel, divided by the spokes, depicts the cyclic periods of manifestation, while the circumference itself signifies the limits of manifestation. This is also symbolized by the *chakras*, often stylized as the lotus, moving the spiritual centres of man, and by the Wheel of the Law and Truth and the Round of Existence, one of the most frequent symbols in Buddhist iconography and one which can even stand as a symbol of Buddha himself as 'He who turns the Wheel of the Law'.

The turning of the wheel depends on the axis, the point at the centre round which everything revolves but which is itself unmoving. This is known as the 'point quiescent', the 'unmoved mover' spoken of by Aristotle in the West. In the East, in Taoism, the unmoving centre represents the Sage who has attained realization and then can move the wheel without himself being moved. It is stillness and peace, being at one with the Will of Heaven.

Time

Time has generally been regarded as an enemy; for the poets, it is 'envious time', 'devouring time', the 'shipwreck of time', and in art it is depicted as the Reaper, either as Cronos/Saturn, or the skeleton with the scythe. The passing of time is shown in the hour-glass and the clock, symbols of the quick passage of mortal life, while the endless cycles of time, the Days and Nights of Brahma, are typified by the turning wheel and the circle, symbols of endless cosmic cycles. In the West, time is generally linear, but in the East it has always been cyclic. While the world is in a perpetual state of change and flux, movement is not necessarily forward; matters can progress in one way and regress in another at the same time. Time both creates and destroys, which explains the symbolism of the Great Mother as Creator and Destroyer, the origin of all life and the bringer of death. As the Moon Goddess, she was always the measurer of time with the moon's variations; as the creative, protective, nourishing mother, she appears as Isis, Cybele, Ishter, Lakshimi, Tara, Kwan-yin, Demeter, Sophia and Mary and is depicted as 'clothed with the sun and having the moon at her feet', the crescent moon and crown of stars being her attributes. As the death-dealing aspect of time she is represented by the Black Kali, Durga, Astarte, Lilith, Hecate, Medea and Circe; she is also the Black Virgin and, in her dark aspect, is often painted in a hideous guise, with serpent-hair or with skulls.

As cyclic time, the Great Mother is also the controller of the seasons with their constant recurrence and the eternal round of birth, growth, death and rebirth. Her day is 'Lady Day', 25 March, when the Spring moon brings new growth and the trees and earth that have seemed dead sprout into fresh green life. With the Summer comes mature growth and Autumn sees both the reaping of the fruits of the earth and the death of the plant in reaping. Winter closes in with what looks like complete death; but the forces of life merely go underground. The seed is stored, or falls into the ground, and lives unseen until Spring comes round once more, for death is only the unseen aspect of life, the change from one form of existence to another. This birth-death-rebirth theme is the basis of all initiation, its archetypal pattern. The initiate, at puberty, dies to the old carefree life of Spring and childhood and takes on the mature life of the adult. In the second death of the Twice Born he, like the seed, descends into the darkness, the dark side of Nature, the descent into hell, to overcome it and rise again to the new life. This is why initiation ceremonies are always held in darkness, or as in ancient religions such as Mithraism, in caves, or in dark huts or the specially constructed belly of some great monster, as in some tribal rites.

The Warp and the Weft

The terrible aspect of the Dark Lunar Goddess, is, as we have seen, associated with spinning and weaving, all Moon Goddesses are spinners and weavers of fate and the web of life in which mankind is ensnared. Spinning and weaving were essentially everyday feminine occupations in the home until the advent of the machine. (Both are now being revived by people who have been through 'civilization' and come out on the other side with a respect for craftsmanship.) The spindle is an attribute of all these goddesses. The spinning whorls signify the revolutions of the universe and the thread spun from them is the thread of life, time and destiny. In weaving, the weft, or woof, is the horizontal plane, the quantitative, the variable human state and the temporal world; the warp is the vertical plane, joining every form of being from the lowest to the highest, from the underworld to the heavens. It is the qualitative, the essence of things, the active and direct. The warp is solar, masculine, the *forma*, while the weft is the lunar, feminine, the *materia*. Woven together they form a cross at each thread and this symbolizes the union of opposites, the perfect relationship of the united male and female principles. The alternating colours of the weft and warp are thought of as the dualistic and complementary forces of the universe, the moon and sun, night and day, negative and positive, *yin* and *yang*. Indeed, in Chinese, the *yin* and *yang* are spoken of by Chuang-hung-yang as 'the to-and-fro motion of the shuttle on the cosmic loom'. Hindu symbolism speaks of Brahman, the Supreme Principle, as 'that on which the worlds are woven as warp and weft'. It also uses the symbol of the spider as the weaver of the web of *maya*, the illusion of the manifest world.

The Egyptian Neith, the Sumerian and Semitic Ishtar and Atargatis and the Greek Athene were all weavers of the fabric of the world, and the Moirai, the Fates, were spinners of destiny. These goddesses of Fate, always grouped in threes, represent not only the phases of the moon; past, present and future; birth, life and death; but are usually made up of two good and one evil or cruel persons, the last of them, like Atropos, being the breaker of the thread of life at the destined time of death. In Scandinavian mythology, Holda and the Norns occupy the same position as weavers of Fate. This symbolism is carried down into the popular world of folk-lore and fairy tale, where we see spinning and weaving always playing a significant and often sinister part and the three fairies becoming involved.

Time, as it passes for the human being, is recorded by the hour-glass, the sun-dial, the water-clock and, later, by the mechanical clock and watch, all of which obviously symbolized the passage of time, transitoriness and the journey of man through the world from birth to death. They also represent the irreversible, always going forward and impossible to put into any reverse movement. This symbolism is linked with man, who finds it extremely difficult to do anything in reverse, to walk or run backwards, read, spell or pronounce words backwards and cannot set a clock into reverse. The only exception to this symbolism is the hour-glass which is turned. Its sand running through signifies first the descent of the soul from the heavens into the world of phenomena and then, as it is reversed, the journey back to the heavens, the return to one's origins. This is the cyclic process of life, depicted by the circular movement of the turned hour-glass and by the circular face of the sun-dial and clock, the cyclic power which involves all life, human, animal and plant alike, giving birth to all, destroying all and then bringing them back to rebirth. When time stops there is the breakthrough to eternity, to enlightenment, as in the mystic experience, the 'timeless moment' or the *nunc stans*.

The 'once upon a time' of myth and fairy tale alludes to the Golden Age, which had access to eternity and in which all things were possible, a time when mankind was wise and lived in harmony, not only with gods and men but with all living creatures, who also lived in peace with each other and spoke the same language. It was the state of Paradise when 'the lion lay down with the lamb'. The nostalgia for this state is expressed by the city-dweller who wants 'to get away from it all' to the peace of quiet places. It is inherent in novels and plays that have the theme of escape to the tropical island, where life is pleasant and easy and food grows on trees, or in the idea of the secret garden, the hidden valley of Shangri-la, all of which are enclosed places, remote and peaceful and the longing for them represents the longing for Paradise Lost. Even the week-end cottage, or car trips into the country, or travel brochures advertising distant and unspoiled places, indicate, in their way, nostalgia for Paradise.

Wholeness

The most significant aspect of the symbolism of the circle is that of archetypal wholeness. It is the whole containing all dualisms, the pairs of opposites which make up the world of manifestation; in it they are contained and united. Again, the most complete and probably the best known representation of this is the *yin-yang* diagram with its interlocking black and white halves, exactly proportioned, but each containing within itself the germ of the other. Each depends entirely on the other and cannot exist except in relationship. Although they are called 'the Contraries', 'the Great Extremes', and the 'Contending Dragons' of the universe, their action upon each other is dynamic, each stimulating the other to harmonious co-operation. They are, at one and the same time, division and unity; they control and regulate the cosmic powers and any imbalance between them brings disruption and therefore 'dis-ease', whether in the physical, mental or spiritual realms. Although the phenomenal world is forever divided into the opposites, day and night, darkness and light, female and male, negative and positive, passive and active, and so on endlessly, their division is not absolute; each can, and does, give rise to the other and the two are ultimately reconciled and resolved in the circle of final unity, when the Two become One.

4. The Cross and the Square

Inseparably connected with the circle and the square is the cross, a symbol so ancient and widespread that no country, age or culture is without it. It appears in innumerable forms. The centre of the cross, the point of intersection of the two arms, like the centre of the circle, square, or any sacred centre, is a point of communication with other worlds and states of being – a cosmic axis.

Most obviously the cross represents the four cardinal points of North, South, East and West, the four seasons of the year and, when in the circle, the four divisions of the cycles of manifestation. But it is also a symbol of archetypal mankind: the vertical axis is the active, masculine, positive and celestial, the horizontal is the passive, feminine, negative and earthly; together they form the whole, the Androgyne. It represents all human potentiality, with the possibility of endless expansion in every direction. This, in itself, also symbolizes eternal life.

Possibly the oldest form of the cross is the swastika; indeed, it is so old that its exact origins are unknown. It has been suggested that it arose from two sticks being rubbed together to produce fire in early times. To support this theory there are representations of the Vedic Fire Queen Arani, whose name means these two sticks, holding them, with four nails and a cup or fosette in the centre, into which a piece of wood was placed upright and twirled violently, by whipping, to produce fire. Others maintain that the swastika was taken from the revolution of Ursa Major in the sky round the pivot of the Pole Star; or that it was developed from the crossing of the Egyptian meander or the Greek key pattern. Alternatively, it has been seen as a development of the Chinese character *chi*, perfection, excellence, renewal of the life force; or, again, that it is the squaring of the circle. But wherever it appears, from India to Iceland, from China to South America, it is always a symbol of good fortune and good luck. The origin of the word we use is taken from the Sanskrit *sv-asti*, 'It is well', or 'Be thou well'.

The Swastika

The swastika is most generally thought to be a sun symbol since it appears with solar gods, fire and thunder gods; but there are two forms of the figure, one revolving clockwise and the other anti-clockwise. These are assumed to be solar and lunar, male and female aspects, and this is supported by the fact that the form appears clockwise with the sun gods and on the heart of Buddha and accompanies solar symbols in most cultures, but is depicted anti-clockwise on images of the lunar goddesses Artemis and Astarte. In China, the two swastikas are definitely *yin* and *yang*: the *yin*, feminine, anti-clockwise, and the *yang* masculine, clockwise. They were frequently used together as a border on ceremonial robes and appear together in the Emperor's ritual sacrificial robes. Interlaced swastikas were also formed into 'mystic knots' and symbolized the mysteries of the universe, inscrutability and infinity. The male *yang* swastika could stand alone and remain lucky, but the *yin* took on the dark aspect if alone and became unlucky. The Nazi swastika was the unlucky form.

On the metaphysical level, the swastika is connected with both the circle and the square and becomes a symbol of movement in a special sense: the movement of life; the action of the Principle in the world, again representing the complementary forces and phases of movement, centrifugal and centripetal, inbreathing and outbreathing, going out from the centre to the circumference and returning to the centre; the Alpha and Omega; beginning and end, and, again, the squaring of the circle.

The swastika can also be formed by the double Z or double S. With the Z form there is the suggestion of the fire symbol, as the two fire sticks, or the Z as a symbol of lightning. The S form, found in Scandinavia, is softer and may be a stylized form of two arms and two legs. This might possibly have some association with the triskele or fylfot, the three-legged emblem of both Sicily and the Isle of Man, which also appeared on ancient coins in Phrygia and which, like the swastika, is a symbol of good luck. It is also an emblem of the Celtic sea god Manannen, associated with the Isle of Man.

In early Christianity the swastika appeared frequently in the catacombs and stood for a symbol of the power of Christ, while in mediaeval times its form as the gammadion—so-called because it

Jain swastikas

Swastika from a mosque in Kashmir

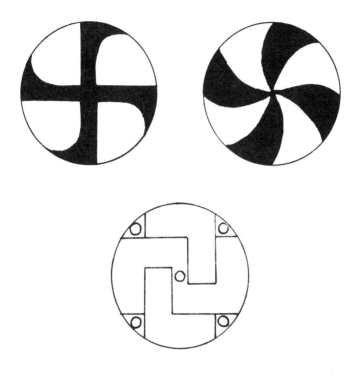

North American Indian swastikas

Four F's forming double swastika Four Tau crosses forming swastika

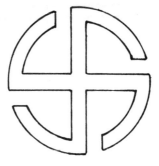

Swastika forming sun circle

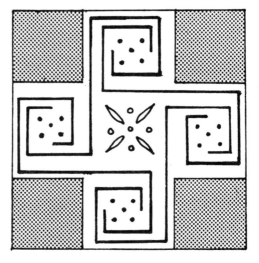

Minoan possible combination of swastika and labyrinth

Egyptian meander forming swastika combined with sun circles

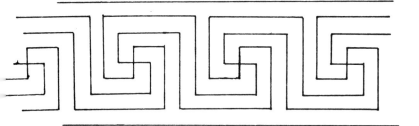

Greek Swastikas

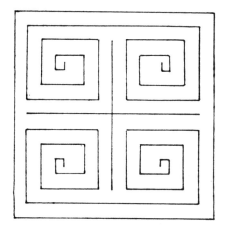

Yucatan Swastikas

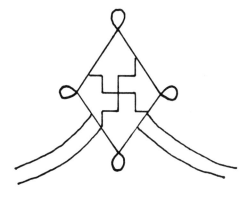

Chinese Swastika

Etruscan Swastika

Bosnian Swastika

Anglo-Saxon spirals forming swastika

Rhodian Swastikas

Hindu Swastika

Persian Swastika

Yin–yang/Female–male

Sicily and Isle of Man

Maori life symbols

was made up of four Greek G's, or gammas—represented not only Christ as the cornerstone but also the four Evangelists, with Christ as the centre. It was used on the garments of the early priesthood and was associated with the Good Shepherd. Later, in England, it was used as a charm on church bells.

Other Forms

There are endless forms of the cross, one of the oldest being the Egyptian *ankh*, known also as the cross ansata, the 'cross with handle'. It is made up of the T cross with the circle above it, thus combining the male and female symbols of Osiris and Isis and forming the union of heaven and earth. Another interpretation of the symbol is that it is the circle of eternity together with the cross of infinite extension; in either case it is a life symbol signifying immortality and 'life to come'. It is also an attribute of Maat, Goddess of Truth, and she is usually depicted holding it in her hand. The Christians adopted this sign when they placed the circle above the cross and put another cross within that circle. But for Christianity the cross also represents death, suffering and sacrifice. The two arms of the cross also signify mercy and judgement and the two natures of Christ. This symbolism is further reinforced by the frequent picturing of the sun and moon on either side of the cross. The wood of the cross was said to have been made from the Tree of Knowledge, which caused the Fall, Christ thus turning it into the Tree of Life or redemption.

The *tau* cross which is mentioned in the Old Testament (Ezekiel 9:4) was found all over Asia and the American continent from ancient times and seems also to have been accepted as a sign of man as, later, Justin Martyr said: 'The sign is impressed on all nature . . . and forms part of man himself.' It appears frequently as a phallic sign, with Priapus and other gods of fertility. It is also the hammer of the thunder gods such as Thor. It is, too, the key to supreme power.

A cross in a circle is a sun sign and forms the wheel of movement, of change and solar power, the heavens, and the wheel of good fortune, while the cross in the square is static and symbolizes the stability of the earth. Among the American Indians, the lodge cross is that of the cross inscribed in the circle and is a world centre, sacred space, the Great Spirit. The cross of the Templars with its rounded ends also suggests the cross combined with the circle and signifies the centripetal and centrifugal forces, while the Maltese Cross with its sharp inward-pointing form typifies the inward-going movement and powers. It also represented the four great gods of Assyria, Ra, Anu, Belus and Hea. The Rose Cross concentrates its symbolism on the centre and is the heart and harmony.

Sometimes the cross and the crescent are depicted together, the crescent then becomes the lunar barque of the Moon Goddesses, the Queens of Heaven, representing the receptive, feminine aspect of life, while the cross is the phallic and masculine element; together they again represent union, heaven and earth.

The St Andrew's Cross of Scotland was also the boundary sign used by the Romans and so signified a barrier. Metaphysically, it is the upper and lower worlds united. The Y, the forked or furka cross, used on Christian vestments to represent the outstretched arms of Christ and also known as the Thieves of Calvary Cross, was earlier said by Pythagoras to be a symbol of human life, the straight stem being the innocence of the child and the dividing arms the left and right hand paths of good and evil, signifying the moral choices of adulthood. Like all crosses, it can also depict the crossroads and the dividing ways in life. Crossroads have always been held to be of great importance, not only as the meeting and dividing of the ways, the meeting place of time and space and the union of opposites, but also as magical and dangerous places where, like the threshold, opposite forces meet. Witches and demons also haunt crossroads. The ancient habit of burying suicides, criminals and vampires at crossroads was to ensure that they became confused and so could not find their way back to their old haunts to do damage to the living. Janus, the god with heads looking both ways, was the god of thresholds and cross-roads.

Variations of the cross could fill a whole volume. There are crosses with the four ends ending in crosses; the crosslet, used by the Gnostics; the Cross Botonnée, with its ends as trefoils or buds, which in Christianity signified Christ as new life and resurrection and is also associated with the budding of Aaron's rod; the Papal Cross, with the triple cross pieces; the double cross, which for the Christians meant both the cross of Christ and the Greek letter X as Christ on the cross (crucifixes as now known were not found before the ninth century A.D.); and the well-known Labarum, also called the Chi-Rho, which was the cross as the Greek letters *chi*, X, and *rho*, R—the first two letters of 'Christ'. In fact, this was older than Christianity and was used in Greek to signify 'a good thing'. And so on almost endlessly.

The four arms of the cross are, obviously, associated with the square, of which they form the diagonals. Both are connected with the number four, the number of the earth, the four cardinal points, the four elements, etc. The square represents the union of the four elements. It is stability, straightforwardness and integrity and represents the solid earth as opposed to the movement of the circle of the heavens. As has been said, it is the basis of fixed buildings, cities, gardens and fields, in contrast to the circle of movement of the tents and circular encampments of the moving, nomadic peoples. The square, or cube, is the base of monuments, both sacred and secular. In the former it represents the earth and earthly levels of existence; it is particularly significant in Hindu symbolism, where it depicts the archetypal pattern of order in the universe, absolute proportion and balanced perfection of form.

Maltese Cross

Potent Cross

Hieracic Cross

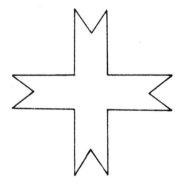

Crosslet

Fichée

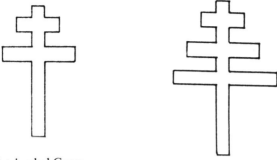

Patriarchal Cross

Papal Cross

The 4-rayed star of Shamash,
later the Maltese Cross

Barbée

Barbée

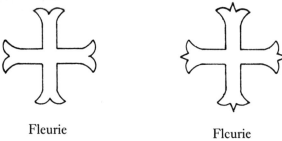

Fleurie　　　　　　　　Fleurie

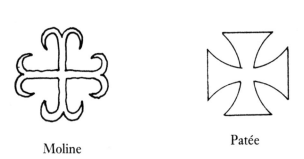

Moline　　　　　　　　Patée

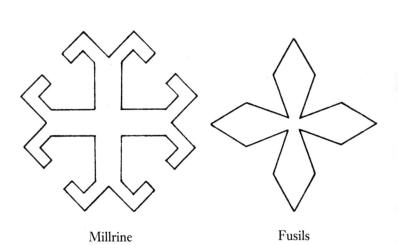

Millrine　　　　　　　　Fusils

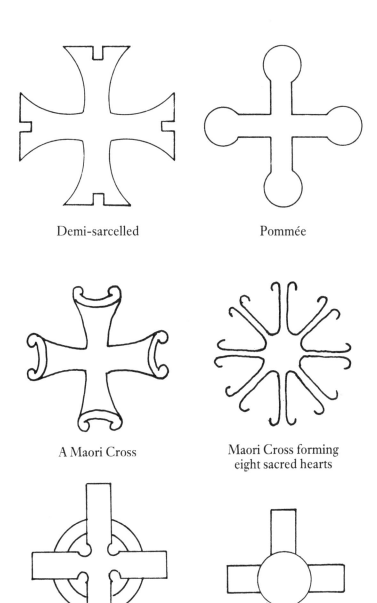

Demi-sarcelled

Pommée

A Maori Cross

Maori Cross forming
eight sacred hearts

Celtic Crosses

Celtic Cross

Botonée

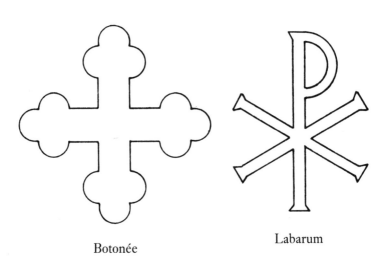

Botonée

Labarum

Amerindian Cross

Directions of winds:

N. the most powerful; all-conquering; the head.
E. the heart; source of life and love.
S. the foot; melting, burning wind; seat of fire and passion.
W. the lungs; gentle wind from the spirit land; the last breath; going out
   into the unknown.

5. The Tree

Much of the symbolism of the cross is shared with the tree, the one often standing for the other. Both are universal symbols representing the axis of the world. They can also symbolize the cosmos itself. The Dying God is always 'hanged on a tree', which is depicted as either a growing tree or a cross. The Tau Cross is called the Tree of Life in Paradise and the Mexicans also referred to the cross as the Tree of Life. For them it was an emblem of fertility and life, sacred to the Rain God. It amazed the Spaniards when they reached America to find the cross, tree, and other symbols they thought of as Christian, already long established in other cultures.

The tree is not only a world axis but a world image; it personifies the whole of the manifest world. Its roots are in the depth of the earth, in contact with the underworld and the waters and so can draw upon the powers of both. The trunk grows into the light and into the world of time and records time by adding a ring to its growth each year. From the trunk the branches spread out and the oneness of the trunk becomes the many, the multiplicity and differentiation of the world of form. At the same time the branches spread upwards and heavenwards and give access to the solar powers, to the realm of the Sky Gods, making it symbolically possible for man to climb up to and communicate with the heavens. To climb a tree, or a notched pole which may represent a tree, as in the case of the shaman's seven-notched birch pole, is equated with passing from one plane of being to another, ascending to the gods, to heaven, or Reality. Climbing is always symbolic of the aspiration to reach higher realms, either to conquer some power to bring it back to earth, or to gain some magical knowledge or treasure, or to attain wisdom. The tree also re-enacts the whole cosmic drama in that it dies and comes to life again; it is a symbol of regeneration and resurrection. This is the dying-to-live principle, while the evergreen tree also signifies immortality and everlasting life.

As well as mediating between the three worlds as it stands, the tree can also take messages skywards when it is used as wood for burning, or as incense, going up to the heavens in the form of flame and smoke.

Often the tree, like the threshold, door or gate, is guarded by a dragon or monster which must be overcome before a treasure or immortality can be gained, and heroes must fight monsters guarding trees with golden apples, or holding the Golden Fleece. This depicts the difficulty of overcoming one's lower mortal nature, as well as all the other obstacles that must be conquered on the way to enlightenment, to regaining the centre.

Trees of Paradise

Paradise has two trees: the first is the Tree of Life, which grows at the centre and signifies regeneration and a return to the state of primordial perfection. It is the tree of unity and transcends both good and evil. From it, at the centre, flows a spring or fountain, giving rise to the four rivers of Paradise, which flow in all four cardinal directions and so form the figure of a cross. The other, the Tree of Knowledge, is dualistic and tasting its fruit enables man to know the opposites of good and evil in the manifest world. Many traditions have a myth of the connection between the Tree of Knowledge and the fall of man from the innocence of the primordial state into the dualistic world and self-consciousness. On the other hand, tasting the fruit of the Tree of Life confers immortality and can restore man to the lost Paradise. One tradition makes the apple the fruit of the fall of Adam and Eve. This is possibly because it was the forbidden fruit of the Golden Age, having been given by Iduma to the gods. In this case, however, the apple was not the fruit of the Tree of Knowledge but that of the Tree of Life, hence the immortality of the gods. In Nordic myth it was the fruit of Freyja's garden and also symbolized immortality. In Celtic tradition the apple, the Silver Bough, was the fruit of Avalon, the Land of Apples, and it had magic powers. Other traditions say that the vine, which symbolizes wisdom, was the Tree of Knowledge (in *vino veritas*), and certainly it is often represented as such in religious art. Immortality can be won either by eating the fruit of the Tree of Life or by drinking the liquid extracted from it, such as wine, the Hindu *soma* or the

Persian *haoma*, both sacred beverages.

The Chinese Taoist-Buddhist Western Paradise has the peach tree at its centre as the Tree of Life. Man, it appears, has always been anxious to make sure of immortality one way or another, and the old Chinese legend of the Monkey and the Peach is a warning that immortality must be won by legitimate means, by striving and spiritual growth, not by stolen fruit. There was once a priest, a mortal, serving in Paradise among the immortals, who fell in love with a beautiful fairy. There was nothing to stop him marrying her except his mortality, and the fact that the fairy was immortal preyed on his mind to such an extent that he longed to attain immortality forthwith. He decided that the best and quickest way would be to steal from the Tree of Life one of the peaches, one bite of which would confer instant immortality. So, waiting until he was under the Peach Tree when no one else was in sight, he stretched up his hand to grasp a peach. But he had forgotten that the Lord Buddha is all-seeing and omnipresent, and, just as his hand closed over the peach, he was changed into a monkey. The monkey-with-peach, which is often carved in jade, or out of peach stones, is thus a symbol of 'vaulting ambition which o'er leaps itself' on the material level and a warning against trying to take any short cuts on the spiritual path.

In nearly all traditions Paradise is an enclosed garden or some other enclosed space such as the Green Isle, or the Islands of the Blessed. An exception to this is the Holy City, the New Jerusalem of the New Testament, though in the Old Testament the original Paradise which man lost was the Garden of Eden. The very name 'Paradise' is derived from a garden, the region round the Persian Gulf and Caspian Sea which was then 'the realm of the rose and the nightingale, of scents and songs'. The Persians called it 'peridaisos', a large, enclosed park. Paradise represents perfection, the Golden Age, the Age of Innocence when everything was spontaneous and free and there was plenty of food available without having to toil for it; a place of peace, rest and happiness. At the Fall, when the fruit of the Tree of Knowledge was eaten, this primordial innocence was lost, heaven and earth were separated, man lost Paradise and with it the power of communion between gods and animals and man, so that they spoke different languages and enmity came instead of understanding and peace. This is the symbolic descent of the spirit from unity into the duality and fragmentation of the world of phenomena; it is the movement away from the centre of peace and perfection to the revolving circumference of change, dispersal and multiplicity; the entry into Time. Then there comes the longing for the lost Paradise and the journey back to the centre, to regain Paradise, to end Time and restore unity.

After Paradise was lost it was, like most sacred places, guarded by monsters or angels with flaming swords and, again, the journey back is fraught with danger and entails trials, testing and arduous discipline and effort.

The Tree, in the world, symbolizes the feminine principle, the protecting, sheltering, nourishing aspect of the Great Mother and it is largely from the tree that this sheltering and protection is provided. Wood gives shelter in the house; at birth in the cradle; in adult life in the bed; in marriage in the bridal bed and at death in the coffin. The cradle represents the cosmic barque, the ship of life in which one sets out to cross the sea of life, and the rocking of the cradle is not only a soothing motion for the baby but also signifies the ship of life rocking on the primordial ocean. Also as a ship of life, the Ark, which was of wood, saved human and animal life from the Flood.

The Great Mother, or Earth Mother, is often represented in art with a tree, sometimes even as it, as in the example of the Sycamore of ancient Egypt. This depicts not only the sheltering qualities but the nourishment provided by its fruits as well. She is always a controller of the waters and, in the tree, is able to draw upon those inexhaustible fertilizing forces and bring them up from the depth of the earth to nourish growth and bear fruit, so assuring survival of man and beast.

The tree can be represented symbolically by a pillar, post, or notched pole; as such it, too, is a world axis which joins heaven and earth and yet holds them apart. Two pillars can typify the two trees of Knowledge and of Life and all the complementary opposites in the world of duality, holding them in tension and balance. This associates them with the *yin-yang* symbolism: the right-hand pillar is usually white, representing the *yang* and the masculine principle, and the left-hand pillar is black, the *yin* and the feminine, symbolizing also spiritual and temporal power, upward and downward movement—in fact, all the opposites. But the two pillars also represent the support of the heavens and so form Heaven's Gate, which is their meaning when they stand on either side of the entrance to a Temple or Church; passing between them and, again, crossing the threshold, signifies entering a new life, leaving the profane world and passing into the sacred.

The Inverted Tree is also a familiar symbol and depicts inverse action; it is also frequently a magic tree. Its roots in the air are the principle which unfolds downwards into manifestation through the trunk and then to the branches; it is the power from on high descending below, with the heavenly and earthly worlds reflecting each other. Sometimes it is a solar symbol, representing the rays of the sun as both power and illumination spreading over the earth. The Sephirotic Tree, which has a vast symbolism of its own, is often inverted, as is the Islamic Tree of Happiness. The Inverted Tree occurs in many traditions: Icelandic, Lapp and Finnish folklore have the same symbol as the Australian Aboriginal witch doctors, who have a magic tree which grows upside-down. It is also present in Hindu symbolism, where the Tree is of great significance. In the Upanishads, the whole cosmos is a great tree and 'Brahman was the wood, Brahman the tree from which they shaped heaven and earth'.

Sacred Trees

Every land and culture has its sacred tree. The Buddhist Tree of Life is the Wisdom Tree 'whose roots strike deep into stability . . . whose flowers are mortal acts . . . which bears righteousness a fruit'. It must never be felled, but the World Tree, on the contrary, must be cut down at the roots since it symbolizes ignorance and worldly desires. The Fig, Pipal or Bo Tree, under which Buddha attained enlightenment, is a sacred tree and represents a Sacred Centre.

In Maori creation myths, the tree forced heaven and earth apart but remains a mediator between them. This is a widespread symbolism. Various trees appear as sacred in Celtic lore. There are the oak and mistletoe of the Druids, representing male and female, solar and lunar powers. The hazel, always a magical tree, was the sacred tree of Celtic groves and, like all nuts, its fruits represented hidden wisdom. As a Tree of Life it grew beside the sacred pool in Avalon; the nuts fell into the waters where the sacred salmon dwelt, and only they might eat the nuts. As a magic-working tree, it was hazel-twigs that Jacob used, in the Old Testament story, when he produced mottled cattle and sheep. The hazel twig is the most usual tool of the dowser.

The ancient Egyptian sycamore, as the Tree of Life, was often depicted as having arms laden with gifts and water poured from a vessel beside it. Hathor is one of the goddesses portrayed as an actual tree. In Greece and Rome the oak occupied the most important role as the tree of the Sky God Zeus/Jupiter, Apollo had the palm, olive and laurel, while the vine was sacred to the wine-god Dionysos/Bacchus.

The Scandinavian Yggdrasil, the ash, has an extensive symbolism, it is the Mighty Ash, the source of life and immortality and the gods meet in council beneath it. Like all cosmic trees it unites all three worlds. Its branches rise to Valhalla and from its roots flows a fountain, source of the rivers and symbolic of the earthly stream of time. Odin's great charger browsed on its leaves and in the boughs the eagle and serpent, as light and darkness, were perpetually fighting for mastery, while the squirrel, a mischief-maker, constantly stirred up trouble between them and ensured that there was no peace in the world. It was on this tree that Odin sacrificed himself for the good of mankind.

The pine, on which the Dying God Attis was sacrificed, and which, via Teutonic tradition, later became our Christmas Tree, was also the sacred tree of Mithraism.

Trees of Life appear as having varying numbers of branches. The Babylonian palm had seven branches, as representing the heavens and the seven planets. The Persian Tree of Life also had seven branches of different metals signifying the seven planets, each depicting the sevenfold history governing a millennium. Hindu and Chinese mythology have a twelve-branched Tree of Life, representing the twelve months of the year and signs of the Zodiac. The Hindu tree has twelve suns in the branches and at the end of the cycle of time these twelve suns will appear all together and shine as a manifestation of the One. The Chinese tree has the Twelve Terrestrial Branches, each with a symbolic Animal of the Constellations. They are divided into six wild and six domestic animals, six *yin* and six *yang*.

So, from a single small seed, has grown the great tree with its deep roots, the massive trunk, its branches and innumerable leaves, flowers and fruits. It is thus symbolically an image of the universe: the many growing out of the One, diversity out of unity and the return to unity in the seed, followed by the re-enactment of the whole cycle of birth-death-and-rebirth.

6. Serpents, Dragons and Monsters

In most Tree of Life myths there is a guardian serpent or dragon preventing man, often by trickery, from obtaining and eating the fruit. Here we have once again the symbolism of wisdom and immortality being difficult to attain. In other myths the opposite occurs and the serpent then tempts the man or woman to find the tree or the fruit for him so that he, too, can win immortality. The serpent is then known as the Tempter, as in the account of Adam and Eve in the Old Testament.

Often the tree is portrayed with a snake at its roots, or, more frequently wound round the trunk; this involves a highly complex symbolism. The snake is masculine, phallic, called 'the husband of all women', and is constantly depicted with the various Great Mothers and when combined with the feminine tree, the two together represent the male-female relationship and balance. But the serpent is also symbolic of wisdom, which is feminine; living underground, the snake is in touch with the feminine powers of the waters and with the underworld, though, like the tree, it emerges into the light. It can also climb the tree towards the heavens, so, again, like the tree, it can be in touch with all three realms and thus becomes a symbol of communication between them and acts as a messenger between gods and men. When the tree and serpent appear together, the tree also represents the world axis and the serpent coiling round it signifies the cycles of manifestation.

Snake symbolism can be confusing as the serpent can be male, female or self-creative; it can represent the lunar, watery, magical power of the Earth Mother, or the solar rays of the Sky Father; it can be good or evil, light or darkness, killer or healer. As a killer it is, of course, death, but being able to cast its skin, and so appear renewed, it is life and resurrection. These dual aspects of the serpent are shown in the Caduceus, carried sometimes by Baal, Ishtar and Isis and always by Mercury, messenger of the gods, who, as Hermes, also represents the power of healing. Here the two entwined serpents depict poison and healing, sickness and health, water and fire: all the opposing forces operative in the universe which yet work in conjunction. This is also the hermetic and homoeopathic 'nature can overcome nature'. In Alchemy, these serpents are the transforming power of male and female sulphur and quicksilver. In Chinese myth, the two forces are represented as *yin-yang* by a brother and sister, Fo-hi and Niu-kua, who are sometimes portrayed as snakes with human heads. It is very rarely in Chinese art that one sees human-animal combinations, but this is one instance: another is the snake-headed human form, which can depict the Year of the Snake in the Chinese Zodiac of the Twelve Terrestrial Branches and their animal symbols.

While in the West the serpent is often represented as evil and a symbol of the Devil, in the Far East it is seldom differentiated from the Dragon, which is beneficent as the Dragon of the Clouds bringing the life-giving rain. It is also wisdom, strength and the supreme spiritual power. It is the great symbol of Taoism: 'The perfect rhythm of the form of the dragon epitomizes all that is contained in Taoist mysticism and its art. It is the ultimate mystery, hiding itself in the clouds, on mountain tops and in deep places; it thus symbolizes wisdom itself—the Tao.' The dragon, like the serpent, has its dual aspects; it is masculine, *yang*, when it is worn on the ritual robes of the Emperor, who was the representative of the great spiritual power on earth. With it stood the phoenix of the Empress, the *yin* power. Together they portrayed the *yin-yang* complementary opposites and the interaction of heaven and earth, the macrocosm and microcosm and all the rhythms of birth and death, of involution and evolution, in the universe. These powers are also depicted as the two Contending Dragons, facing each other, symbolizing the Two Great Powers in tension and interdependence.

In the monotheistic religions, the dragon is usually evil and is fought against by some hero, such as St George. The dragon frequently guards some treasure or maiden, symbolic of hidden wisdom, a theme which is found in myth, legend, drama and fairy tale and which also typifies the age-old conflict between the powers of good and evil, light and darkness, the seeming death of vegetation in winter and its rebirth in spring. On the psychological level, it is also man overcoming his own dark nature. One of the exceptions to the evil dragon in the West is the Red Dragon of Wales, who is much nearer the Eastern dragon as a solar power.

In Christianity the dragon and serpent are spoken of as one and the same: 'that old serpent', the Tempter, and it also signifies death and darkness: in the Old Testament 'the place of dragons' was also connected with death. The fight between the Archangel Michael and the dragon is older than Christianity, which, as in so many other instances, adapted pagan myth to fit its teaching. St Michael is the ancient Sun God who overcomes the dragon or serpent of darkness. On the other hand, the serpent can represent Christ as wisdom, and the serpent on the cross is Christ raised up on the Tree of Life. The evil serpent is Satan, Lucifer, the Devil, while Tertullian says Christ was called 'the good serpent'. When the snake is associated with the Tree of Life it is beneficent; with the Tree of Knowledge it is evil.

Buddhism has two different interpretations in its snake symbolism. There are three creatures at the centre of the Round of Existence: the pig as greed, the cock as carnal passion and the snake as anger, these being the three main sins which bind mankind to the world and to the round of illusion. But the serpent sometimes represents Buddha himself, who changed his form into that of a *naga*, or serpent, to help to heal people at a time of disease and famine.

The healing aspect of the snake also appears in Celtic myth when it is associated with the healing powers of the waters and the Celtic horned-god Cernunnos is often depicted as a horned serpent; here it is a symbol of virility and fertility; it is also an attribute of Bridgit, the Celtic Great Mother.

Other examples of the serpent as evil and manifesting the powers of darkness are when it is pictured with the eagle, as in the branches of the Yggdrasil, or with the stag; these are two solar powers fighting against and overcoming darkness; the victory is depicted as the eagle having caught the serpent in its talons or the stag trampling it underfoot. On the other hand the winged serpent or dragon symbolizes the union of opposites in the world, the union of spirit and matter.

The well-known Plumed Serpent of the Aztecs is solar and as a combination of bird and snake it also represents the powers of wind, rain, thunder and lightning and is seen with all rain and wind gods. It is also the powers of ascension, the breath of life, knowledge, and is a messenger between gods and men.

Animal Combinations

The combinations of birds and beasts, such as the Gryphon, which has the head and talons of an eagle and the body of a lion, in some cases are beneficent, here symbolizing the great solar powers, strength and wisdom. Christianity, however, depicted the gryphon as the Devil, but later Dante said it denoted the two natures of Christ. In other cases, for example the Basilisk or Cocatrice, a bird and serpent combination, the creature is wholly evil and at enmity with all good. Some pose a definite threat and have to be slain by the hero, as in the story of the Cretan Minotaur, half-bull, half-man, who symbolizes both a guardian of the centre and primordial chaos. It was slain by the culture-hero Theseus, who then finds the centre, abolishes a threat to others and restores law and order. Other monsters are neutral, such as Capricornus, which appears in the Zodiac as half-fish, half-goat and represents the winter solstice; it is also a form of the ancient Babylonian god Ea-Oannes. The Centaur, another sign of the Zodiac, is half-horse, half-man, and is also known as the Archer. It signifies the whole man, comprising both his animal and spiritual nature, while his bow and arrow are symbols of power and control, with the exact angle of 45° typifying the perfect use of that power. Combinations also signify freedom from the usual conventional rules of the world and introduce other possibilities in creation. Fearsome monsters may represent the dark and terrifying powers of nature and the dangers to be encountered in the psychic realms on the spiritual path. They, too, are frequently guardians of the threshold or of treasure, either material or spiritual, and have to be overcome

7. Animals

It has been said that man is a symbolizing animal and has to come to terms with his animal nature. Animals symbolize the emotional and instinctual life in man, primitive urges that must be transcended before the spiritual realms can be entered. This is why so many legends, myths and stories contain animals or monsters which must be slain or tamed before a desired goal can be reached or a treasure found. But animals that accompany man, or help him on adventures or quests, represent the different qualities and aspects of his own nature, or those instinctual and intuitive powers which are often of assistance when reason is inadequate or fails. Stories and fables of friendship with animals, or of saints and sages communicating with them, are symbolic of the Golden Age, of Paradise, and of re-entry into that state. On a lower level, wearing bird or animal skins or masks, as in shamanistic rites, not only endows the wearer with animal wisdom, but also reproduces the primordial unity that existed before the Fall. It is also recognized that animals have a sixth sense, which man has now largely lost. Adopting animal guise was believed to restore this faculty. Animals are also symbols of fertility and teeming life.

Pairs of animals, when one is solar and the other lunar, signify the two contending but complementary powers in the universe, the best known examples being the lion and the unicorn, bull and bear, or bull and boar. As we shall see, many animals are capable of an ambivalent symbolism, being masculine and solar in one context and feminine and lunar in another.

The Dog
Of all animals, the dog has been most closely associated with man as 'man's best friend' and it is not surprising that it has become a symbol of fidelity and watchfulness. It is also one of nobility, since

dogs and falcons were the property of nobles. Plutarch says that dogs symbolize 'the conservative, watchful, philosophical principle of life'. But the dog was more than a domestic, hunting, guarding, working companion of man: it was always a 'guardian of the threshold', a guardian of treasure and of boundaries between this world and the next. In this capacity it was a psychopomp, one who conducts souls to the other world, and it also accompanies messenger gods, such as Hermes/Mercury. It is an attribute of Anubis, the dog- or jackal-headed Egyptian god, and helps him to keep the sun on its right path. Cerberus, the three-headed dog of Greek myth, guards the threshold of the underworld. The Teutonic-Scandinavian Woden/Odin had two dogs, as well as ravens, as counsellors who brought information to him from far and wide.

The dog is also associated with war and with gods of war and destruction. Hecate had her 'dogs of war', which she let loose on the world. A dog usually accompanies huntresses, such as Artemis and Diana, and Mother Goddesses, for example Belit-ili and Ishtar, both of whom are sometimes portrayed as a whelping bitch. The Mother Goddesses are also known as the Lady of the Beasts, Queen of Animals and goddesses of the hunt, war and death; lions or dogs often support, or sit by, their thrones.

Although usually a solar animal, the dog can become lunar when it is the companion of these moon goddesses, or when it is connected with the underworld. In China, it was *yang*, solar, and a bringer of good fortune in the day-time as the Celestial Dog, when it drove off evil spirits, but as a guardian of the night watches it became *yin*, lunar, and destructive. It was then associated with meteors and eclipses, at which time the dog goes mad and bites the sun or moon, taking a piece out of it, and has to be driven off with fire-crackers and much noise. The Hindu Indra, a god of war, is accompanied by a hunting dog, and Yama, god of the dead, is sometimes depicted as a dog with four eyes, while his two watch-dogs represent the chill and gloom of dusk and pre-dawn—times when hostile powers are at large. This also occurs in Greek and Celtic symbolism.

The Greeks seem to have adopted contrary attitudes to the dog. On the one hand it is, according to Homer, shamelessness, and the Greek pejorative term 'cynic', or dog-like, implies impudence. On the other hand, the dog Sirius, as all-seeing vigilance, accompanies the hunter Orion as his faithful companion, and, at the Feast of Artemis, on 25 March (Lady Day, feast of the Lady of the Beasts), dogs were garlanded, made much of, and given a great feast. Also, when associated with Aesculapias, the dog heals through rebirth into new life and its fidelity survives death.

The only traditions that hold a consistently poor opinion of the dog are the Semitic and Islamic. In both cases the dog is regarded as unclean and is a symbol of impurity. In ancient Sumero-Semitic times the dog was associated with the scorpion, serpent and all reptiles as evil, baleful and demonic. On the other hand, in Phoenician art, the dog accompanied the sun and was also an attribute of Gala, the Great Physician, and of the Accadian Belit-ili, whose throne was supported by dogs, or who had a dog sitting by her.

Among the Parsees, in Zoroastrianism, the dog holds a special place. Contrary to Islamic practice, it is carefully looked after, has its place in the community life and a special significance in funerary ritual, since it accompanies the dead at a funeral. It is thought that it was probably regarded originally as a psychopomp and to support this belief is the fact that if two people are buried together, such as a mother and child dying at childbirth, two dogs must accompany the funeral cortège.

Christianity, in contrast to the Judaism from which it sprung, adopted a favourable attitude to the dog and took it as a symbol of fidelity and vigilance, also as representing the Good Shepherd, since it looked after the flock. In this aspect, it also became a symbol of a bishop or priest. Christian legend has several examples of the faithful friendship of dogs, for instance St Roch, who was fed by his dog, while the St Bernard is a well-known emblem of that saint.

A black dog is associated with witches and sorcery, demonic powers and death and often appears as a ghost-warning of impending death. Cats and dogs, as witches' familiars, can be disguises of witches as rain-makers—hence 'raining cats and dogs'.

The Cat and the Horse

As a naturally nocturnal animal the cat is almost universally connected with the powers of darkness. Like the black dog, the black cat can also be a witches' disguise and so it was always regarded as unlucky and augured misfortune, or a change for the worse. It is only in modern times that it has become a good-luck omen. Having eyes which vary according to the power of the light, the cat can also represent the varying power of the sun and the waxing and waning of the moon. As lunar, the cat is an attribute of the moon goddess Diana and the Egyptian Isis, but it was only during the ascendancy of Set, the god of darkness and evil, that it became sacred in Egypt. The Scandinavian Freyja has a chariot drawn by cats. In China it is a *yin* animal, as nocturnal, and is supposed to have powers of transformation. It is avoided as a sign of unlucky change and a black cat is an omen of misfortune. Christianity also stresses its dark aspect and it represents laziness, lust and the Devil.

Like the black dog and cat, the black horse is ill-omened; it is funerary, heralds death and symbolizes chaos. It was said to appear during the twelve days of chaos between the old and new year. White horses are ambivalent: they can be solar when they appear with sun gods, usually drawing the sun-chariot, or lunar when they represent the humid element as the steeds of the sea gods and are thus connected with the chaos of the primordial waters.

The winged horse is always white or golden. As well as being solar power, it signifies the swiftness of thought, the intellect, reason, dynamic force and nobility. The Greek Pegasus typifies the possibility of passing from one plane to another. In Buddhism, the winged or cosmic horse 'Cloud' is a form of Avalokitesvara, who, in Chinese and Japanese Buddhism, changes into the goddess Kwan-yin or Kwannon. In secular Chinese symbolism the horse is the heavens, fire, *yang*, and is at any time a good omen. Its hoof, not its shoe, brings good luck. When the horse and dragon appear together, the dragon is the supreme symbol of heaven and the horse then becomes the female mare, earth, and *yin*. In the decorations used in marriage ceremonies, the stallion depicts speed and accompanies the lion of strength for the bridegroom, while flowers represent the bride and feminine nature.

The Hindu cosmic horse, Varuna, was born of the waters, and when Vishnu, sustainer and indwelling spirit of the universe, appears on earth as an avatar, for the tenth and last incarnation, his 'vehicle' will be Kalki, a white horse, and he will bring peace and salvation to the world. Ten is the number of fulfilment and plenitude, here representing the restoration of the Golden Age at the millenium. This symbolism of the white horse is paralleled in the Apocalypse, where St John sees the heavens open and beholds a white horse. 'He who sat upon it is called Faithful and True'.

In Celtic mythology, Epona, the Great Horse, is the goddess-mare, an earthly and underworld deity. She was later adopted into the Roman pantheon. But the Celtic horse could also be solar as virility and fecundity. In Greek myths, too, white horses are both solar and lunar, the former as the steeds of the sun-chariot of Phoebus, or the latter as the white horses of Poseidon, god of the sea and controller of the humid principle and of earthquakes and springs.

The horse is frequently associated with the World Tree, to which the gods tethered their chargers; thus, the horse partook of the potency, wealth and power of the gods. But it also typifies the instinctual animal nature, as when it is the animal half of the centaur. It can also have magic and divinatory powers. With the bull it is one of the best known symbols of fertility and both were used as sacrificial animals, representing sky and fertility gods. The sacrifice of the October Horse, towards the end of the year, signified the death of death.

There is also some subsidiary symbolism attached to the horse. As instinctual animal nature it must be controlled and tamed; here the rider or driver represents the mind, which curbs animal instincts with bit and bridle. Both these accoutrements typify control, endurance, forbearance and temperance. In this context they are attributes of Nemesis, goddess of retributive justice. In Christian art the bit and bridle sometimes accompany the figure of Temperance. In Hindu symbolism the horses are the physical life-forces, while the reins are the will and intelligence. The two wheels of the chariot are heaven and earth, joined by the axis, and the turning of the wheels represents cyclic time and cycles of manifestation.

In the West the horse-shoe, as distinct from the horse-hoof in China, is a well-known symbol of good luck when turned upwards. In this position it is crescent-shaped and so represents the moon and the lunar goddesses. This equates it with the horns of power and protection, also with the receptive cup and nourishment.

The Bull and the Cow

It may seem strange that the bull can be anything other than a masculine, solar animal, depicting the generative force of the sky gods and the king as representative of the divine power. But, like the horse, it can also be allied to the earth and the humid principles in nature. So we find the bull, ridden by solar, warrior, sky and storm gods, portraying the fertilizing power of sun, rain and thunder; but, as the white bull, it is also the mount of moon goddesses, such as Astarte and Europa. Here this depicts the taming of the masculine and animal nature by the feminine power, as does the tethering of the solar gods' horses to the feminine tree and the hanging or crucifixion of the Dying God on the tree.

The bull is a universal symbol, everywhere representing strength, speed, fertility and the generative powers. Winged bulls are guardian spirits and the bull-man, particularly common in Sumero-Semitic tradition, is usually a guardian of treasure, of a centre, doors or thresholds as sacred places. He can also ward off evil powers.

In Buddhism the bull signifies the ego and is also an attribute of Yama, god of the dead. Both the ego and death must be overcome ultimately. The opposite obtains in Celtic tradition, where the bull-gods embody divine power and strength. For the Druids, the bull was the sun and the cow the earth.

The Egyptian bull, Apis, was an avatar of Osiris and the bull was worshipped under the form of Mnves or Merwen and was sacred to Ra, the sun god. In Greek and Roman myth, both the masculine and feminine symbolism are apparent: as an attribute of Zeus/Jupiter, the sky god, the bull is solar, masculine, but it is also connected with the humid, feminine force, as associated with Poseidon and Aphrodite. The Hindu Agni, the Mighty Bull, is a form of Indra and the bull Nandin is a vehicle of Siva, guardian of the West.

The original Iranian tradition in Zoroastrianism has the bull as the soul of the world. It was the first created creature and when slain by Ahriman, Lord of Lies and Darkness, the germ of all later creation rose from its soul. Famous in Minoan art, the bull is the Great God and was sacrificed to the earthquake god. It tossed the earth on its horns and its roaring was heard in volcanic eruptions. Bull sacrifice was the central rite in Mithraism and it represented life through death and victory over man's animal nature. In Judaism the Bull of Israel is the might of Jahveh; but in Christianity the bull merely denotes brute force.

With the bull as the generative forces of sky and rain, the cow represents the productive power of the earth and is an aspect of all Mother and Moon Goddesses, symbolizing nourishment, abundance and procreation. But the horns are the crescent moon, so the cow is both earthly and celestial. She is probably best known as Hathor, who, in Egyptian art, is depicted as wearing horns on her head. As the sacred animal of Hinduism the cow, Prithive, the earth, the all-embracing, appears with the bull of heaven. The Scandinavian primordial cow, the Nourisher, sprang from the primeval ice which she then licked to produce the first man.

Horns are always symbols of power; growing out of the head, the power of the life-force of the head was ascribed to them. They also typified dignity, nobility, protection, royalty and divinity. There are various horned gods, notably in Celtic lore, and they represent warriors and the combined powers of humans and animals. This was the significance of the horned helmets of the Vikings. Storm gods were also depicted as wearing head-dresses with horns. But horns occur on both bulls and cows, so they are both solar and lunar, the horns of the sky gods and the lunar crescent of the moon goddesses.

The Pig and the Boar
The pig, with its large litters, was always a fertility symbol, hence the 'lucky pig' charms mean prosperity. On the other hand, the pig is always associated with gluttony, lust and uncontrolled passion, so it becomes unclean and depicts vice. Its symbolism varies between the fecund, maternal aspects of the sow, the Earth Goddess, and the greed and ignorance of its physical characteristics. This is particularly evident in Buddhism, where the Tibetan Adamantine Sow is the Queen of Heaven, the Moon and fertility; but, as we have seen, the pig occupies a place at the centre of the Round of Existence, where it represents greed and ignorance. The Celtic Moon Goddess is also the Sow, the Shining One.

Like the bull, the boar can be both solar and lunar, good and evil. It is solar as the masculine force and as a brave fighter, a warrior, but lunar in that it is a dweller in the forests and the swamps and so is associated with the dark and watery elements. The Druids called themselves 'boars', possibly because they often dwelt in the forests as solitaries. The Celts venerated the boar as a sacred animal and connected it with prophecy, magical powers and the protection of warriors. Scandinavian warriors wore boar masks and boar tusks on their helmets. This put them under the magical protection of Frey and Freyja, who both rode boars. The boar was sacrificed to Frey at Yuletide and the ceremony of bringing in the boar's head arose from this.

Sheep, Lambs and Goats

Noted for their silliness, sheep are naturally taken as an example of helplessness, stupidity and unintelligent following of a leader. As a flock following a shepherd (in the East the shepherd leads and the flock follows), they are equated with Christians following Christ, an illustration used by Christ himself. But the concept of the Good Shepherd is much older than Christianity and occurs in Sumerian, Iranian, Orphic, Hermetic, Pythagorean and Tibetan traditions. He is also a saviour and a psychopomp and, in this connection, is sometimes associated with the God of the Dead; both can carry the staff and crook as their emblems. In Egypt, Ra was 'the Shepherd of All Men'. The Sumero-Semitic Tammuz, a moon god, was a shepherd and protector of flocks. The Iranian Yima, the Good Shepherd, possessed the solar eye and could confer immortality. The Hindu god Siva was a herdsman and Krishna lived with herdsmen and shepherdesses. The Tibetan Chenrezig, 'the All-merciful Good Shepherd' is incarnated in the Dalai Lama. In Greece, Orpheus Boukolos is the Herdsman, the Good Shepherd, his attribute, as with Christ, being a kid or lamb carried on his shoulders. Pan is a herdsman and Hermes/Mercury is a shepherd of souls.

If the sheep is regarded as a generally unattractive animal, exactly the opposite applies to its young. The lamb, born in the New Year, or in spring, when everything is fresh and unjaded, is a natural symbol of innocence and purity. It is also equated with gentleness, meekness and the unblemished, all characteristics which made it suitable as a sacrificial animal. Its religious symbolism is largely Judaeo-Christian, for the Lamb Without Blemish was the coming Messiah. This was carried over into Christianity when Christ was crucified as the sacrifice of the Lamb, which represents Christ as being both sacrificed for the sins of the people and as triumphant at the resurrection. In Christian art, Christ carrying a lamb is the Good Shepherd caring for his flock, or having found the lost lamb that went astray, redeeming the sinner. The lamb with the cross denotes the crucifixion, while the lamb with the pennant or flag portrays the resurrection. Depicted with a book and seven seals, it is the apocalyptic lamb, Christ as Judge at the Second Coming. When the apocalyptic lamb has seven horns and seven eyes it signifies the seven Gifts of the Spirit. A lamb with a hill, from which flow four streams, typifies the Church as the hill and the four streams as the rivers of Paradise and the four Gospels. John the Baptist with a lamb is an allusion to the forerunner pointing to the coming of the Messiah. When a lamb is portrayed with a lion it is an expression of the paradisal state before the Fall when 'the lamb lay down with the lion', before sin and enmity entered the world, a state which will occur again when Paradise is regained. It is also connected with the symbolism of the sage and the saint, the enlightened person who has regained the Centre, or Paradise, and in whom there is no conflict.

The fleece of the sheep or lamb has a special symbolism since it is equated with the fat of the animal. This was always regarded as its life-force, and, by extension, it represents all life-sustaining produce and hence longevity.

Goats have a mixed significance. The male goat shares with the bull, horse and boar the attributes of masculine virility and generative power, but, living in high places in the wild, it also takes on an aspect of superiority and can change places symbolically with the gazelle and antelope, which are largely lunar animals. The female goat denotes feminine fertility and abundance. In Sumero-Semitic art the goat appears with Marduk, the sun god, and with hunter-goddesses and there is also the strange goat-fish with the head, horns and forefeet of a goat and the tail of a long fish, who represents Ea-Oannes, Lord of the Watery Deep, and the dual powers of land and sea. The goat-fish is also a form of Capricornus in the Zodiac. The goat and ram are both attributes of the Vedic fire god Agni, who rides a he-goat.

For the Greeks and Romans, the goat embodied virility and

Goat-Fish

lust. It was sacred to Zeus, who was suckled by the she-goat Amalthea, whose skin later became the aegis, the protector and preserver, and whose horn was the cornucopia, symbol of Amalthea and of abundance. The wild goat was sacred to Artemis and was also an attribute of Dionysos, while Pan and his satyrs had the legs, horns and beard of the goat. Christianity equated it with the Devil, the damned and all sinners. At the Last Judgement mankind will be divided into sheep and goats, the saved and the damned. The scapegoat represents Christ taking on and carrying the sins of the world and is usually depicted as wandering in the desolation of the wilderness.

The Ass and the Donkey

'Silly ass' is regarded as the ultimate in condemnation of stupidity and it is stupidity and obstinacy which are most frequently associated with the ass or donkey, but it can also typify humility, patience and peace and it is yet another fertility symbol among animals. The Egyptians equated the donkey with inert evil power as an emblem of Set in his bad and typhonic aspect, while for the Greeks it was taken as sloth and infatuation. It was sacred to Dionysos and Typhon as a brutish form and was also sacred to Priapus as a fertility symbol, but became malefic when associated with Cronos/Saturn. Silenius, associate of Dionysos, is sometimes portrayed as riding on an ass in a drunken state. On the other hand, in Hebrew tradition, kings, judges and prophets rode on white asses. For Christianity the donkey is associated with the nativity, the flight into Egypt and the triumphal entry into Jerusalem, but at other times it is synonymous with the Devil.

Hares and Rabbits

Hares and rabbits are largely interchangeable in their symbolism; both are lunar, live in the moon, and are associated with lunar deities. The hare in the moon is almost universal, appearing in such widely different traditions as the Chinese, Hottentot, Mexican, Indian and European. Being closely connected with the moon, the hare represents rebirth, rejuvenation and resurrection. As lunar 'light in darkness' it is also intuition. It can act as an intermediary between men and lunar powers. On the other hand, its nature makes it an appropriate symbol for such qualities as fleetness, timidity and crafty wisdom. It is particularly important in American Indian lore where the Great Hare is the Hero Saviour, Hero of the Dawn, father and guardian, creator and transformer. He is the Great Manitou who lives in the moon with his grandmother and is 'provider of all waters, master of winds and brother of the snow'. He is also one of the well-known Tricksters, symbolizing the nimble mind which outwits dull physical force.

The Buddhist hare-in-the-moon was put there by Buddha to honour it because once, when Buddha was hungry, the hare offered himself as a sacrifice and jumped into the fire. It also appears with the crescent moon in Hindu and Buddhist iconography. Celtic hunter and moon deities were associated with the hare and were often depicted holding it in the hand. For the Egyptians it was also lunar, but had the added significance of being connected with the dawn. Graeco-Roman mythology made it an attribute of Hermes/Mercury and it was thus a messenger animal, though it had another significance, arising from the rapid breeding powers of the rabbit—that of fertility, fecundity and lubricity. In this connection, cupids were often portrayed with hares.

In China the hare-in-the-moon holds a pestle and mortar with which it mixes the elixir of immortality. Figures of hares, or white rabbits, were made for the celebration of the moon festival. Being lunar, the hare is, of course, a *yin* animal. It is the guardian of wild animals. The Jews regarded the hare as an unclean creature and some of this symbolism has come over into Christianity, where it is equated with fecundity and lust; but the white hare, portrayed at the feet of the Virgin Mary, signifies triumph over the passions. In Europe, in Teutonic and Anglo-Saxon beliefs, the hare, or rabbit, played an important part, as will be seen when reference is made to the Easter festival. In Europe, the white hare symbolizes snow and the March hare, when it capers about wildly at mating time, is madness.

The Fox, the Frog and the Rat

Another creature whose temperament gives it an obvious symbolic character is the fox, universally regarded as an embodiment of slyness, cunning, craftiness and trickery. The only variation in this significance comes from China and Japan, where the fox has magic powers of transformation and can appear in any guise to wreak mischief or to incarnate the ghosts of dead souls, but this, too, involves trickery. Being nocturnal; it is *yin*.

Always associated with and living in the watery element, the frog is lunar and a fertility symbol. Two of its characteristics make it a representation of resurrection and a renewal of life; it partakes of the creative powers of the waters, the medium for all life, and it has a moist skin, which contrasts with the dryness of death. Its connection with the waters made it important for the Celts, who called it Lord of the Earth. The Egyptian Green Frog of the Nile was new life, fertility and abundance, as well as strength out of weakness. It was an attribute of Isis, but particularly of Hekt, as the embryonic power of the waters; she was protector of mothers and the new-born. The Hindu Great Frog supports the universe and is the dark, undifferentiated *materia*. The Greeks and Romans made it an attribute of Aphrodite/Venus as fertility and licentiousness, but it was also a symbol of harmony between lovers. Christianity has the frog as resurrection, but the toad is the repulsiveness of sin.

Long before modern medical knowledge, the rat was known to be a carrier of the plague, so it was inevitably equated with death and the underworld and is taken as wholly evil in the West. Only in India has it any beneficent symbolism where, in Hinduism, it represents prudence and foresight and is the steed of the god Ganesha, who successfully overcomes obstacles and difficulties. The Chinese connect the rat with meanness and timidity; mice, too, are regarded as timid, retiring and insignificant, poor and lowly.

8. Birds and Insects

Birds, in general, are a symbol of the soul: spirits of the air; the spirit freed from the body; or they can be a manifestation of divinity. Their powers of ascension make them natural symbols of all that rises or is associated with the upper regions of the air and heavens, and thus with aspiration and transcendence. Flying upwards confers on them the power of trafficking between this world and the next, so they are frequently messengers of gods and angels; they often accompany the hero figure of myth, legend and fairy tale on his adventures or quest and give him secret and supernatural advice, hence 'a little bird told me'.

Hens, Ducks, Geese and Turkeys
Domestic birds, however, have a more mundane significance. The hen is the outstanding example of the maternal instinct in caring for its young; she also represents providence and procreation. A black hen joins the black dog and cat as a witch's agent or an aspect of the Devil, while a crowing hen typifies feminine domination or a bold, forward woman, so alarming that 'a whistling woman and a crowing hen frighten the Devil out of his den'. In Christianity, the hen with chicks depicts Christ with his flock, adopting a simile of his own in saying how often he had wanted to gather the people of Jerusalem to him as a hen gathered her chicks.

The duck, on the other hand, has given rise to more metaphors and similies than symbols, such as 'a dying duck in a thunderstorm', 'water off a duck's back' and so on. Such symbolism as it has is Eastern and Amerindian. In the latter case, it can be a mediator between the spirits of sky and water; for China and Japan it represents married happiness and fidelity, felicity and beauty. A duck and drake depicted together are the union of lovers, mutual happiness and consideration. Sometimes the ducks are portrayed as joined together, with only two wings between them—the closest form of marital union and happiness.

The symbolism of the goose is more widespread than that of any of the other domestic birds. It is predominantly solar, since the goose was said to follow the sun on migration, and it can also change places symbolically with the white swan, which is entirely solar. The goose is the 'breath bird', the wind; it is also watchfulness, since it gives instant and loud warning of the approach of strangers. The sacred geese, kept in Rome and associated with Mars as war god, Juno as Queen of Heaven and Priapus as fertility, were said to have saved Rome by giving the alarm at the coming of invaders. Both Greeks and Romans saw the goose as an attribute of war gods, but it was also an emblem of the solar Apollo and the messenger god Mercury, of Eros as love and Peitho as goddess of eloquence and winning speech! The Celts also regarded the goose as an attribute of war gods. But it was probably Egyptian and Hindu symbolism that gave it the greatest importance. In Egypt, the Nile Goose, the Great Chatterer, was the creator of the world as it laid the Cosmic Egg from which emerged the sun, Amon-Ra. The goose was also an emblem of Seb, or Geb, the Earth God, and depicts love; it is, too, an emblem of Isis, Osiris and Horus. The Hindu wild goose, or gander, is a vehicle of Brahma, the great creative principle. It also denotes freedom, devotion and spirituality, learning and eloquence. The Ham-Sa is depicted as either a goose or a swan and is the most notable of the goose-swan interchanges.

In China, the goose is again connected with the solar, *yang* power, and is a messenger bird, bringing good tidings. Like the duck, it represent conjugal happiness, but it also signifies seasonal change in Autumn, and, although solar, it is frequently shown in Chinese and Japanese art as associated with the autumn moon. In the West, geese are eaten at Michaelmas and Christmas, times which are connected symbolically with the waning power of the sun in Autumn and its rising power after the shortest day at the end of December.

Like tobacco and the potato, the turkey is a comparatively recent import to the Old World from the American continent. There it was the sacred bird of the Toltecs, the 'jewelled fowl', and was the food for festivals and ritual thanksgiving occasions, a symbolism which has been taken over in the States for Thanksgiving Day, and generally in England as a Christmas bird.

The Dove

Another bird associated with the home, and often kept as an ornament or pet, is the dove, which has a worldwide symbolism of peace and gentleness, especially when it is depicted with the olive-branch of peace. It is also the spirit of light, the soul, and is sacred to all Queens of Heaven. Sacred doves were also connected with funerary cults. But the dove's significance is ambivalent in that it is regarded as a bird of innocence and chastity, but in some cases it also represents lasciviousness, particularly as the pigeon. In the Old Testament it typifies innocence, simplicity, meekness and embodies the souls of the dead. In the New Testament and in Christian art it is used to portray the Holy Spirit, the Annunciation, baptism, peace and harmlessness. A flock of doves depicts the faithful; seven doves represent the seven Gifts of the Spirit; a dove with a palm branch is not only peace but also victory over death; a white dove is a saved soul, as opposed to the black raven of sin. In Sumerian and Hebrew tradition a dove was sent forth from the Ark, at the time of the Deluge, and, according to the Old Testament account, brought back the olive-branch of peace between God and man.

In Egyptian iconography, the dove sits in the branches of the Tree of Life and appears with the fruit of the tree and with vases of the Waters of Life. For the Greeks and Romans, the bird was a symbol of love, especially as an attribute of Venus, a Queen of Heaven, and was also renewal of life. Zeus was fed by doves; Athene has the dove with the olive-branch; Adonis and Bacchus have the dove as an emblem of love and passion. In Islam the Three Holy Virgins are often represented as pillars surmounted by doves. The pillars are here an aniconic form, that is, not having human shape, of the women. Both China and Japan regarded the dove as a symbol of longevity, deference and orderliness, but in Japan it is also sacred to the god of war.

The Stork and the Crane

Together with the eagle and the ibis, the stork is a destroyer of reptiles, creatures which are always baleful in significance, so anything that kills them is beneficent and solar; but of the three, the eagle alone remains completely solar, since the ibis and stork get their living in swamps and by rivers, in the watery element. As we have seen, this element is always connected with creation, life being embryonic in the waters; so the stork, in close association with the embryonic, is a bringer of new life: hence babies being 'brought by the stork'. It also symbolizes the coming of new life in the spring and is invariably a good omen; it is good luck to have a stork's nest on the house.

Also a bird of the waters, the crane has an extended symbolism in the East. It is solar, a messenger of the gods and an intermediary between heaven and earth. It carries souls to Paradise and it denotes longevity, vigilance, prosperity and high office. In China it is 'the Patriarch of the Feathered Tribe' and in Japan it is 'Honourable Lord Crane'. It is usually depicted with the sun and the pine trees in oriental art. In direct contrast, in Celtic mythology, it is sacred to the king of the underworld and heralds war and death.

The Eagle

The strength and magnificence of the eagle naturally associate it with might, authority and royalty. The attribute of all sky gods, and usually interchangeable symbolically with the hawk and falcon, it is also the spiritual principle, soaring upwards, inspiration, the element of air. As solar, it is in constant conflict with evil or underworld powers and, as has been said, one of the most frequent representations of the eagle is battling with the serpent or holding a snake in its talons—depicting the war between light and darkness, good and evil. But although in conflict, together the eagle and serpent represent a totality of spirit and matter, and hence ultimate cosmic unity. The fight between eagle and lion, or eagle and bull, in which the eagle is invariably victorious, signifies the triumph of the spiritual over the material, mind over matter.

Double-headed eagles are attributes of twin gods and symbolize double power, omniscience and omnipotence. In Alchemy they depict the male-female Mercury, while the crowned eagle and lion are wind and earth, quicksilver and sulphur, the volatile and the fixed principles.

The eagle-feather head-dress of the Red Indian Chief is an expression of the Great Spirit, the Thunder Bird, and the eagle is a mediator between sky and earth. For the Aztecs, the eagle was celestial power, the rising sun, the devourer of the serpent of darkness. The Hindu eagle is the Garuda Bird, on whom Vishnu rides, and which is at war with the Nagas, the serpents. In Scandinavian mythology, the eagle appears in the boughs of the Yggdrasil, the World Tree, as light and, again, is in conflict with the serpent of darkness. For the Greeks and Romans, the eagle was the lightning-bearer of Zeus/Jupiter, a symbol of spiritual

Red Indian Feathered Sun

power and, for the Romans particularly, the power of the Emperor, and the Roman eagle was seen wherever the Roman army
and colonists went.

There were strange beliefs about the eagle. It was held to be
able to soar up to the sun and gaze at it without blinking; it was
also thought to renew its plumage by flying up to the sun and then
plunging down into the sea. Christianity used these notions as
symbols of Christ gazing at the glory of God and Christ rescuing
souls from the sea of sin. The eagle as inspiration was used
particularly to represent the inspiration of the Scriptures, hence
its use as a lectern in churches.

The Vulture and the Owl

In odd contrast to the solar-masculine eagle, the vulture was
thought at one time to be entirely female, with the hawk or falcon
as the male, so that vultures represented the feminine, maternal
principle, caring for their young and providing protection and
shelter. On the other hand, they were also symbolic of destruction
and voracity, but as scavengers they represent purification and are
workers for good. In Egypt, Isis, having once assumed the form of
a vulture, gave it the significance of maternal love and good works.
Hathor is sometimes vulture-headed and Maat wears a vulture

head-dress. In Graeco-Roman myth, the vulture was sacred to Apollo but also ridden by Cronos/Saturn.

As a bird of the night and a bird of prey, most religions and myths associate the owl with darkness and death, while Christianity also equates it with the Devil as the power of darkness. The notable exceptions to this gloomy symbolism are the Amerindian and Graeco-Roman civilizations, in which the owl is a bird of prophecy and wisdom. It is an attribute of Athene/Minerva, and it is from this source that the West derives the notion of 'the wise old owl'.

The Swan and the Wren

We have seen that the swan and goose can join in the same symbolism and even change places, but, in addition to this, the swan has a considerable significance of its own, notably in its 'song'. It was supposed to sing a particularly sweet and plaintive song as it died. This gave rise to the 'swan song' as a metaphor for death or some final act, and the sweet singing was also equated with the poet's song. The swan thus became the bird of the poet, hence the reference to Shakespeare as 'the Swan of Avon'. In this poetic connection it also became the bird of solitude and retreat. Combining the forces of air and water, it is a bird of life, of the dawn, and is predominantly solar. Celtic swan deities are all solar and beneficent and possess the healing powers of both the sun and the waters. The swan has great powers of transformation, so that in myth and fairy tales kings, princes and princesses often take, or are changed into, the form of swans. In a swan with a gold or silver chain round its neck, one may instantly recognize some transformed royalty or the supernatural appearance of a divinity.

Graeco-Roman myth gave the swan an amorous significance in the story of Zeus/Jupiter turning himself into a swan to woo Leda, and in being sacred to Aphrodite/Venus. It was also the solar bird of Phoebus/Apollo. In Christianity, the white swan is an emblem of the Virgin Mary, while singing with its dying breath typifies the resignation of the Christian martyrs. The golden cosmic egg of Hinduism was laid on the waters by the divine bird and from it sprung Brahma, who is often depicted as riding on a swan. The Ham-Sa, either a swan or a goose, but more usually the former, is 'that pair of swans, who are Ham and Sa, dwelling in the mind of the Great'. They are carved on temples and portray the perfect union towards which celestial beings fly; they are also Breath and Spirit.

Strangely, one of the smallest of birds, the wren, is known as 'King of the Birds', 'the Little King', but its symbolism is ambivalent as it can take the place of the dove as representing the soul or spirit, while on the other hand it can also denote a witch, and so becomes malefic. It is usually considered extremely unlucky to kill a wren, but in England and France it used to be hunted at Christmas, killed and taken round hanging from a pole. Houses were visited in procession and largess expected. Finally, the bird was buried in the churchyard as symbolizing the death of the old year.

The Bee

Among insects, bees are probably the most symbolic, universally typifying industriousness and order; but, being winged, they share with birds the ability to carry messages from this world to the world of spirits and the ancient habit of 'telling the bees' of any important event or death in the family was a means of sending the news to the souls in the next world. Also, like birds, they can be equated with the soul and hence with immortality. In olden times it was believed that bees were self-fertilizing, so they signified chastity and virginity.

Nearly every tradition has its bee symbolism. In Hindu iconography, a bee on a lotus depicts Vishnu; blue bees on the forehead depict Krishna and the ether; bees as combined sweetness and pain form the bow-string of Kama, god of love. In ancient Egypt, the bee stood not only for industry, but was a giver of life and therefore of immortality. It also denoted royalty and was an emblem of the Pharaoh of Lower Egypt. The Greeks believed that the souls of the departed could enter bees. The Mother Goddess was known as the Queen Bee and her priestesses were *melissae*, the Bees. The officiants at Eleusis were Bees, and bees were associated with Pan, Priapus and Zeus, also with Demeter, Cybele and Diana: they were the 'birds of the Muses', bestowers of eloquence and honeyed words. Among the Romans, although Virgil calls bees 'the breath of life', a swarm of bees denoted misfortune, while a headless bee averted the evil eye.

Islam equates the bees with the faithful, with intelligence, wisdom and harmlessness and ibn al-Athir says that: 'Bees benefit fruit blossoms, practise useful things, work in day time, do not eat food gathered by others, dislike dirt and bad smells and obey their rulers; they dislike the darkness of indiscretion, the clouds of doubt, the storms of revolt, the smoke of the prohibited, the water of superfluity, the fire of lust.' The Celts believed that bees held secret wisdom which they derived from the underworld. Christianity thought of the bee as diligence, order, prudence, and associated it with chaste virgins and the Virgin Mary. As a body the hive represented the ordered and pious life of the religious community; here the bee is the Christian and the hive the Church.

Other Insects

The ant is another symbol of industriousness, ordered community life and virtue, but it also carries a suggestion of unintelligent submission and subordination, so that we speak derogatively of any vast urbanization or totalitarian state as 'a veritable ant heap'. The emphasis with the ant is on work for work's sake and an inability to appreciate or use leisure, as opposed to the carefree grasshopper who sings and plays the summer through but stores nothing for the winter months. Here the ant is held up as a model of thrift and forethought, but in fact fable is unjust to the grasshopper, who often benefits the ant in providing it with scarce and much-needed moisture since it can pierce the stalks of plants and liberate the juices. The ant, incapable of doing this, avails itself of the grasshopper's superior powers. The Chinese have an affection for the grasshopper and cricket and keep them in little grass-made cages, delighting in their cheerful noise. They symbolize good luck, abundance and virtue. In diametric opposition, the Hebrews typified the grasshopper as a scourge, probably equating it with the locust. The golden grasshopper of the Greeks depicted nobility and the aristocrat.

The spider has already been referred to, but it may be added that in some Oceanic islands the Old Spider is the creator of the universe. Its association with the powerful Great Mother Goddesses and the Fates accounts for making it unlucky to kill a spider. Although the spider can be baleful, it is good in that it preys on the fly, which is always associated with disease, corruption and evil. The Phoenician Beelzebub, Lord of the Flies, is the agent and power of destruction, death and putrefaction. Demons are often portrayed as flies, which can be the embodiment of evil supernatural power.

9. Fishes

While animals live on the element of land and birds in the air, the element of water has been regarded by most traditions as being the origin of all life. The primordial waters are chaos, the formless, containing the potential of all forms and all possibilities in manifestation. They are essentially the creative element of the maternal, the Mother of All Things, so that it is not surprising that fishes are associated with all aspects of fertility and creation and have a universal, varied and rich symbolism.

We have already noted that fish was eaten at the feasts of the Mother Goddess on her day, Friday. Fish, like bread and wine, was a sacramental meal of the mystery religions and was associated with the ritual worship of all moon goddesses of the waters and gods of the underworld. As fecundity, life created, renewed and sustained, the fish was also phallic.

Fish deities riding on fishes or dolphins represent the independence of motion in the waters, potential and all possibilities. Fish swimming downwards depict the movement of the involution of the spirit, and, swimming upwards, the evolution of spirit-matter. Two fishes indicate spiritual and temporal power. Three fishes, often portrayed intertwined, or with three bodies sharing one head, are an almost universal symbol of the trinity of divine power. This latter symbol is found in iconography in such widely different cultures as ancient Egypt, Mesopotamia and the Celtic, Persian and French.

In Hinduism, the fish is a vehicle of Vishnu as Saviour, in his first incarnation, when he saved mankind from the Flood and founded a new race of men at the beginning of the present cycle. A golden fish is a symbol of Varuna, who controls the power of the waters, while the fish in general typifies fertility and wealth. In Buddhism, it appears on the 'Footprint of Buddha' and indicates

Chinese pair of fishes

Three fishes as the trinity of divine power

freedom from restraint and emancipation from the desires and attachments of this world. Buddha is a Fisher of Men.

Christianity used fish symbolism extensively. The Early Fathers were called *pisciculi* and fish were equated with the converted, swimming in the waters of life. The Apostles were Fishers of Men. In Christian art, fish, with wine and a basket of bread, are a commemoration of the Feeding of the Five Thousand and represent the eucharist at the Last Supper. The fish also signifies baptism, immortality and, from Jonah's emergence from the whale, resurrection. Christ was depicted by the rebus ICHTHUS , a fish, as *Iesous Christos Theou Huios Soter* (Jesus Christ Son of God Saviour). The three fishes intertwined, or with one head, was adopted from earlier religions as denoting baptism under the Trinity.

Salmon and trout and the dolphin were associated by the Celts with their sacred wells and healing waters as symbolizing the foreknowledge of the gods, and Nodon was a Fisher God. In Chinese 'fish' and 'abundance' are homophones, so the fish represent wealth, regeneration and harmony, while a pair of fishes, usually carp, so frequently seen in Chinese art, portray the joys of union, marriage and fertility. The Mother Goddess, Queen of Heaven, Kwan-yin, has a fish as an emblem, so had the T'ang dynasty; but a single fish can also depict a solitary, lonely person, such as an orphan, widow or widower. The carp has a special literary significance as it stands for literary eminence as well as typifying perseverance in the struggle against difficulties, a symbolism taken from its long and hard journey up stream to spawn. When it has achieved its goal the carp is said to have 'leaped the Dragon Gate' and become a dragon, hence this is also a complimentary term for a scholar successful in the difficult literary examinations. In Japanese, 'carp' is a homophone for 'love', so is equated with it as well as being an attribute of Kwannon. It is also an emblem of the Samuri, as courage, endurance and resignation to fate.

In Judaism, fishes are the faithful in their true element of the waters of the Torah. The old Jewish Passover was in the month of Adar, the Fish, and fish was the *coena pura* of the meal of the Sabbath, food of the blessed and symbol of the heavenly banquet in the future life.

The Sumero-Semitic Ea-Oannes, Lord of the Deeps, the fish-goat god, was served by a priesthood who wore fish-head head-dresses, which later became the mitre of the Christian bishops, and fish was the eucharistic meal of the priests of Atargatis, for whom sacred fish were maintained in fish ponds at her temples. Her son was Ichthys, the sacred fish. The fish was both a masculine, phallic symbol, as an emblem of Ea and Tammuz, and feminine fertility and creativity, as associated with Atargatis, Ishtar and Nina.

Among the Greeks and Romans the fish was a symbol of love and fertility, an attribute of Aphrodite/Venus, but also of Poseidon/Neptune as the power of the waters. Orpheus was a Fisher of Men. The fish also had a funerary significance and indicated new life in the next world; it was an offering for the dead in the worship of Adonis.

In the Zodiac, the twin fishes of Pisces, facing in opposite directions, represent the arcane substance, and the fish-goat is Capricorn.

The Dolphin and the Whale

The dolphin, which has often been reported as a friend and guide to sailors and a saver of the shipwrecked, assumes this symbolism in the spiritual world and is a psychopomp and guide to souls. It is the King of Fishes, sea-power, safety, swiftness. Two dolphins, depicted as swimming in opposite directions, signify the duality of nature, while the dolphin with the anchor portrays the opposites of swiftness and slowness, the moving and the static. Both the Greeks and the Romans attributed the powers of the psychopomp to the dolphin in guiding souls across the sea of death to the Isles of the Blessed. For the Greeks, it was both solar and lunar in its significance since it was connected with Apollo Delphinos as light and the sun; but it was also used for the representation of the feminine, watery principle and the womb on account of the similarity of sound between *delphis* and *delphos*. It has an amatory association as an emblem of both Aphrodite and Eros. Thetis, the sea-goddess, rides naked on a dolphin. The Sumerians used the dolphin as an alternative to the fish representations of Ea-Oannes and it is an attribute of Ishtar and sacred to the Syrian Atargatis.

Christianity adopted the dolphin as a symbol of Christ as saviour of souls and as the bearer of souls over the waters of death. In Christian art, a dolphin with a ship, or an anchor, depicts the Church guided by Christ. This sometimes replaces the ship, or ark, of salvation and rebirth. The dolphin can also take the place of the whale as denoting resurrection.

The whale naturally symbolizes power, the power of the Cosmic Waters, and thus regeneration, both cosmic and individual; but it is also equated with the all-engulfing grave. The 'belly of the whale' is a place both of death and resurrection. In the Old Testament, the symbol of Jonah and the Whale carries on the tradition of being swallowed by a whale, or any big fish or monster, as an initiation rite, in which death is first experienced, then, after the traditional three days of the dark of the moon, the new man emerges from the cavern of initiation into the light of new life and rebirth. But Christianity equated the whale with the Devil; its jaws are the gates of hell and its belly is hell.

Conch Shell

The Shell

Also associated with the sea and the power of the waters is the
shell. It is uniformly a feminine symbol of this power, the
universal matrix, the moon, birth and regeneration, love, marriage and fertility. In funerary rites, the shell signifies both the
journey across the sea of death and resurrection into a new life. It
is an emblem of Aphrodite/Venus, 'born of the sea', who is often
depicted as riding, or standing on, a shell. Association with her
also makes it a love symbol. For the Christian, the shell denotes
the waters of baptism and shells are sometimes used for sprink-
ling the water on the baptized. The scallop shell is associated with
St James and is one of the symbols of the pilgrim. In China, the
shell and the pearl are *yin*, the watery element, with jade as the
yang heavenly principle. The shell also signifies a good life in the
next world.

The conch shell has a considerable symbolism of its own. Its
convolutions suggest the rising and setting sun, the lunar spiral
and the movement of the waters. Like any shell it is an attribute of
Vishnu, Lord of the Waters in Hinduism, and it was the conch
shell from which the primordial creative sound OM issued, which
was the word made manifest. Buddhism also adopts the conch as
a symbol of primordial sound and uses the shell ritually, as a
trumpet, in worship. Here it denotes the voice of Buddha
preaching the Law and proclaiming victory over the world,
samsara. The conch is one of the Eight Symbols of Good Augury
in Chinese Buddhism. For the Greeks and Romans it is an

emblem of Poseidon/Neptune and Triton. The Tritons, drawing the chariot of Poseidon, blow conch shells. In Mayan art, the conch appears frequently in any symbolism associated with the waters. In Islam it is the ear which hears the Divine Word.

10. Flowers and Fruit

It will have become obvious that the Great Mother dominates the symbolism of all that is concerned with creation, growth and the maintenance of life, as well as the forces that give rise to and control life, the waters, the earth and the moon. Hers is a highly involved symbolism as she is not only the Earth Mother, the *tellus mater*, but also the Moon Goddess, equated with the waxing and waning moon, and called the Queen of Heaven. The moon in turn is associated with the tides and the power of the waters, so she controls these also. Thus, as both the waters from which all things are born, and the fertile earth, she is the *prima materia*. She is the Mother of God, since from her was born the incarnate saviour, both in the material world and in the experience of the individual soul or psyche. She is the Bride of God since she, as the soul, must unite with the Divine. She is the daughter of God since God gives rise to all things. She is the archetypal feminine, the origin of all life and form. In myth she is the Virgin Mother who bears the Dying God son. The word 'virgin' here simply means pure, free, untrammelled, not tied by the bonds of matrimony. She symbolizes all the phases of cosmic life, uniting all the elements, the heavens, earth and waters. Of her, in her aspect as Isis, it was said: 'I am all that has been, and is, and shall be, and my veil no mortal has yet lifted.' She is the great mystery of life and death and is known by many names in all ages and traditions.

The Ear of Corn
As the Earth Mother, all trees, plants and flowers are associated with her in the cycle of birth, life, death and rebirth. Pre-eminent among the plant symbols is the ear of corn, or wheat. It is not only one of her chief attributes but also of her son, the Dying God, who is also the Corn God, associated with the awakening of life in

spring, as well as with the death of winter, when the seed of the ear of corn falls into the cold earth to die before it germinates and is reborn into new life. The Dying God of vegetation signifies this ever-recurring cycle of death and rebirth, of dying in order to live—the eternal return. He always combines the masculine and feminine principles of the Sun, or Father, the god whose rays warm and fertilize the earth, and the Earth Mother, who nourishes and brings forth the seed. He is thus frequently depicted as a beautiful, feminine-looking youth, or as a her-maphrodite. He never attains to maturity but is killed by, or dies on, a tree (the feminine power). He is always born miraculously of a virgin. He is the young beauty of spring, the death of summer-past, the decaying vegetation of autumn and the death-sleep of winter. He wakes again and is reborn as the year turns; the sun gains power and life is once more renewed.

An ear of corn was the central symbol of the Mysteries at Eleusis, which were focused on the worship of the fertility goddesses Demeter or Ceres (from whom our word 'cereal' is derived). Corn was also sacred to Artemis and Cybele and bread was eaten sacramentally at their rites and those of other earth and moon goddesses (the bread was often made into round cakes or buns and marked with a cross, as is now done in the case of our Hot Cross Buns). The roundness of the cake depicted the moon and the cross was the four lunar quarters. In sacramental meals, bread is associated with wine and the two together are tokens of the balance of man's efforts and skills in agriculture, providing both food and drink. The bread, from the corn, is equated with the Earth Mother, the feminine principle; wine is associated with the fiery and masculine aspect; bread is solid, wine is liquid; wine is associated with divinity, bread with the earthly, so the two together symbolize the union of opposites. In Greek mythology, Demeter, the Earth Mother, represented the corn while Diony-sos, the young and beautiful Dying God, was the god of wine. In Christianity, the bread and wine of the sacrament were adopted to signify the dual nature of Christ, with the wine as his divine nature and bread as his earthly incarnation.

Flowers are frequently associated with various gods, especially those who were sacrificed, when flowers sprang from their blood on the soil. Anemonies, flowers of sorrow and abandonment, grew from the blood of Adonis, the violet from the blood of Attis, the hyacinth from that of Hyacinthus, and roses from the blood of Christ. Eastern divinities emerge from the lotus, since it represents both the light of the sun and the power of the primeval waters, the matrix. Brahma, Buddha and Horus all symbolically emerged from the lotus. Venus, originally a garden deity, is associated with both the vine and the rose of passion.

The Violet and the Rose

Other qualities of flowers are well-known: the violet, with its hidden beauty and sweet scent, portrays modesty and humility. In Greek mythology, as well as being sacred to Attis, it is the flower of both the gentle Io and the fierce Ares, god of war, who, however, was a god of agriculture before he changed his mythological character and became a war god, disliked by other gods for the senselessness of war.

The rose has a wide and ambivalent symbolism. The white rose is purity, perfection, innocence and virginity, but the red rose is exactly the opposite, standing for earthly passion and fertility. The rose can represent both time and eternity, life and death. It has always been the flower of mystery: the 'heart of a rose' is synonymous with the unknown; the whole rose is the pleroma. As depicting life, it is a symbol of Spring, resurrection, love and fecundity; as death, it typifies transitoriness, mortality and sorrow. Both these aspects were present in its use in the ancient funeral gardens of the Romans. The element of mystery in the rose has invested it with a symbolism of secrecy. Thus, a rose was incorporated as a decoration on the ceilings of council chambers to remind those sitting under it of the need for secrecy and discretion (hence the expression *sub rosa*). The association of the rose with passion also connects it with wine, seduction and sensuality, but also with happiness, when it is 'roses, roses, all the way ...'. But the thorns of the rose mean pain, blood and martyrdom.

Red and white roses placed together represent the union of opposites, the blending of fire and water. Red signifies the masculine, the King; white is the feminine, the Queen; red the sun, white the moon; red as gold, white as silver. But since the blending of the two opposites into a final union must mean the death of the individual ego in the greater life of the One, any red and white flowers together can symbolize death. The golden rose is always perfection, while the blue rose represents the impossible or the unobtainable.

Rose/Rosette

Cypriot

Mexican

Greek

Saracen

The Lily and the Lotus

Christianity uses a considerable amount of flower, plant, tree and garden symbolism. The white violet, white rose and lily-of-the-valley all depict the purity of the Virgin Mary, while the cyclamen, with its red spot, portrays the bleeding of her heart (it is also called the 'bleeding nun'). The pink carnation signifies the Virgin's tears and her motherhood, while the lily, either as the 'madonna' or arum, or sometimes the narcissus, is perhaps the flower most associated with her. Its straight stalk is her godly mind, its hanging leaves are humility, its whiteness stands for purity, its fragrance denotes divinity.

The lily, sometimes in the form of the iris, is sacred to all Virgin goddesses as both Mother and Maid, the chaste virgin, Queen of Heaven, and the Mother Earth. The lily is, in the West, the counterpart of the lotus in the East, though the lotus carries an even greater and more profound symbolism. Like the rose, the lotus has both masculine and feminine attributes and is both *yin* and *yang*, since it grows out of the *yin* lunar, watery element into the light of the sun, the *yang*. Like the lily it is purity, beauty and feminine perfection. The lotus also expresses spiritual unfolding; starting with its roots in the slime, it grows upwards through the dark waters and its flowers, floating on the waters, reach the light of the sun and the air of the heavens. Its roots represent indissolubility; the stem is the umbilical cord which keeps man attached to his origins and the flower takes on the form of the sun's rays. The seed-pod, which completes the cycle, is the fecundity of creation and returns the seed to the original waters. The same plant bears buds, flowers and seeds at the same time and so is associated with past, present and future, which, in turn, means totality. In China, it is especially the flower of the beautiful and serene Kwan-yin, Queen of Heaven and Goddess of Compassion. The lotus also appears with ancient Hindu and Egyptian sun gods and with Semitic moon gods and goddesses. As both masculine and feminine, it is a symbol of the light and fire of the sun and the feminine lunar powers of the waters of creation, the two interacting to produce perfection.

The Primrose and the Marigold

In the West, the primrose has a strangely mixed symbolism. It is both purity, youth and innocence on the one hand and pertness on the other. It is also associated with frivolity and dalliance: 'the primrose path of dalliance treads, and recks not his own rede'. In

Lotus

Lotus with Swastika. Cyprus

Greek

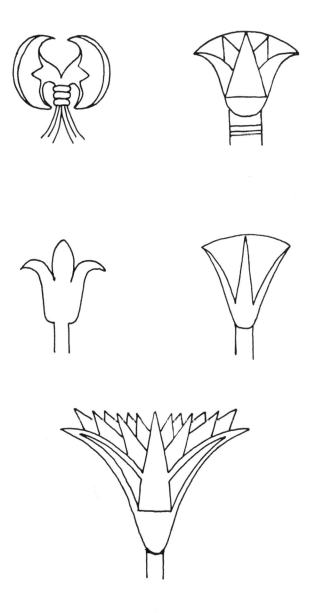

Egyptian forms

Celtic lore it is a fairy flower, as is the cowslip. Certain flowers have the power of warding off fairies, witches and their spells, such as St John's-wort and verbena. As fairies are particularly fond of stealing human babies, in order to bring them up as their own, and put a changeling in the cot instead, it is as well to know that branches of rowan or hawthorn, as well as their flowers, are effective in keeping out ill-disposed spirits, either from the house or the cattle-byre, where they are prone either to steal the cattle or to milk cows dry.

The marigold simply means fidelity in the West, but in the East it is more significant. It is longevity and 'the flower of the ten thousand years', ten thousand being synonymous with the uncountable, the endless. The marigold is used extensively on Buddhist shrines and in Hinduism is the flower of Krishna.

Paradise and the Gardener

Flowers and gardens are associated with the abode of the soul, the 'better land', Paradise, and with this goes the symbolism of innocence and happiness, which, in turn, connects them with childhood. Fragility and evanescence are other qualities that link flowers with childhood and innocence, but also equate them with transitoriness of life. Five-petalled flowers especially symbolize the Garden of the Blessed; they also represent man with the five senses and five extremities. In the East, where there are six senses, mind being the sixth, the six-petalled flower, particularly the lotus, depicts the whole cosmos.

The gardener is always the Creator, who grows the life-giving tree with its nourishing fruits and flowers of beauty. The enclosed garden, as well as being Paradise, is a symbol of virginity and in Christianity it is specifically associated with the Virgin Mary. It also stands for the sheltering, enclosing, feminine principle. Miniature gardens, particularly in Taoism, are earthly copies of Paradise. The Romans planted enclosed gardens on the graves of their dead and here, too, the gardens were regarded as the counterpart of Elysium. They were often planted with vines as well as roses, the latter typifying eternal spring and the former representing life and immortality, but having the added practical use of providing wine for the libations offered to the dead. Relatives and friends would hold banquets in honour of the dead in those gardens, forshadowing the feasts in the Elysian Fields.

ii. Creation and Initiation

Among the great contraries, the negative and positive, the Two Great Powers as Taoism calls them, water and fire are probably the most significant. Both are creative and destructive, both a source of life and death, both generative and purifying forces. All waters are associated with the Great Mother, the feminine principle, and with birth. They also represent flux, endless change, and so carry life away as Time 'like an ever-rolling stream'. Death is spoken of as crossing a river, or crossing the waters. Crossing any waters symbolizes change from one state or plane to another. But while the waters wash away, they also purify and give new life, a symbolism which also applies to fire. Water and fire are not only purifiers but both are objects of necessity and longing, though at the same time of fear and danger. Man perishes more readily from lack of water than from lack of food, and fire is the great consolation and necessity for warmth and cooking; but both are as easily death-dealing as life-preserving. They are opposites and antagonistic, but like most opposites, complementary. When they work together, they produce powers as great or greater than their own. Both have the qualities of instability and great mobility; both are world-creating and world-destroying elements. (The world having once been destroyed by water, many traditions have a prophecy that the next destruction will be by fire.) As complementary forces they are the darkness of the waters and the light of fire; the cold, tide-controlling moon, the depth of the ocean with the fiery heat of the sun and the height of the heavens. We speak of 'the sea of death' and the sun sinks into the ocean at night; its light is swallowed up and darkness prevails, but rebirth comes with the dawn and the sun rises out of the sea once more, which now becomes the sea of life.

There is always this union of opposites in creation, of death and rebirth. In Alchemy, they are represented as the King and Queen, Sol and Luna, who, existing as opposites in the realm of duality, ultimately through dissolution and rebirth become the Androgyne and achieve primordial perfection. This is symbolized by the male-female figure or the two-faced head of the King-Queen, and in other traditions it is shown as the bearded goddess or the effeminate young god. The Androgyne is the One, in which all contraries are resolved and spiritual unity is attained. In the case of traditions in which man's first ancestor was androgynous, this is also a symbolic return to one's origins, the perfect state from which man fell into dualism.

After the Fall and the loss of Paradise, man's longing and aim was to find that lost state of bliss and the original unity again. To do this he had to be re-created, re-born. Traditionally, man has three births. The first is physical, when he enters the material world; the second is at initiation, when he is born into the cultural or spiritual life of the community; and the third is at death, when he is reborn into the next world. Each stage is a dying to the old state and rebirth into a new; the whole completes a cycle.

The birth at initiation can take many forms. In tribal societies, boys and girls are initiated into adult life in the tribe at puberty and go through ceremonies which vary with the form of symbolism adopted by the particular community, yet all are uniform in expressing the idea of death to the old life and birth into the new. In religions, the ceremonies and symbolism are spiritual in nature; in the tribe they are cultural as well as religious. In Greek culture boys, *epheboi*, went through an initiation which marked the end of childhood and the beginning of manhood; both sexes had their mystery religions into which they were initiated if proved fit.

Baptism

An age-old and almost universal form of initiation and acceptance into a cult or religion is baptism. It signifies regeneration, a death and rebirth, again with the initiate dying to the old life and being born into the new life of the select society of the Twice-born. The novice dies to the old nature and, purified, is born into the new divine nature. Baptism is most usually by water, but can also be by fire, wind or blood. The Mithraic initiate was baptized in the blood of the sacrificial bull, blood being the rejuvenating force and symbolic of the life-principle and the soul. Baptism by fire burns away the dross of the old nature and restores primal purity in regaining Paradise which, since lost, has been surrounded by fire, or guarded by angels with flaming swords. Wind blows away the chaff and, like fire, is a force of purification and transformation; it is also the vital breath of the universe and the power of the Spirit.

The most frequently adopted form of baptism, however, is by water, again a great purifier and creator; but water also dissolves all forms and differences and reduces everything to the primordial state of formlessness, to the state before the creation, before the birth of the world, so that man reverts to the pre-natal state in the womb of the waters before being born again of the waters of baptism. To enter the waters, as in baptism by immersion, is to go back to the beginning and start again, hence the flood stories found in every civilization and religion. In creation myths, when life dawned, it emerged from the ocean, or some great god or founder of a race came out of it, or from across the seas. Then, when the world became degenerate and man turned to wickedness, the waters were let loose to wash away the old state, to abolish all forms and to give birth to the new. The past was wiped out, washed away, dissolved in the waters of the flood and a new creation established, a new world born.

Early Christian baptism closely parallels this symbolism. It also included ideas of death and the reunion of the Second Adam and Eve in the sacred marriage. This was the birth of the new man, the child of God within the Mother Church, the baptized having 'become as little children'. Now, in Christian churches there are two initiatory ceremonies; first baptism, which is both a sacrament of purification and of entry into the Church, a rite which usually takes place in infancy and is combined with name-giving which confers individuality on the child. (Christianity, holding the doctrine of original sin, insists that the new-born child is already in a state of sin; this is linked with the superstition that it is lucky for a baby to cry at baptism as it denotes 'the Devil going out'.) The second ceremony is a corroborative initiation, which, at about the age of puberty, is the candidate's own choice. It is therefore called Confirmation, when the individual is admitted, as an already baptized member, into the full rites of the Church.

Marriage Symbolism

After initiation at puberty, entering the adult world carries the possibility of marriage, a rite which is symbolically the reconciliation of opposites, the interaction between contrary but complementary forces. The Sacred Marriage, the *hieros gamos*, was

Male–Female unity

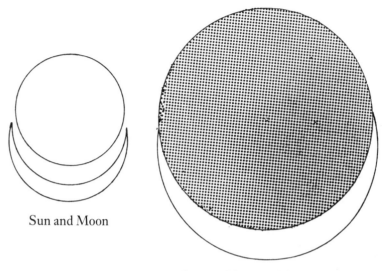

Sun and Moon

Moon and Sun

celebrated ritually in ancient religions between the God and Goddess, Priest and Priestess, King and Queen, as typifying the mystic union between Heaven and Earth, Sun and Moon, often symbolized by the bull as the sun and the cow as the moon, or the solar lion and lunar unicorn. In Alchemy it is the *conjunctio*, the union of the masculine sulphur or gold and the feminine mercury or silver, the King and Queen. In Christianity it signifies the union of the Soul, the Bride, with Christ the Bridegroom.

Marriage symbolism remains basically similar all the world over. First there is the betrothal in which some token of unity is exchanged. This is most usually a ring, which is a symbol of binding but also signifies the personality; so the exchange of rings, or the bestowing of a ring, is to transfer power as well as to plight a troth. The ring also represents power and dignity; it shares the symbolism of the circle as completeness, fulfilment, continuity and, by extension, imperishableness. This completion and fulfilment, expected of marriage, binds to a new state, to a new life, but it also expands in the fullness and completeness of that life. The ring, together with the crown and sceptre, is a royal symbol, and the bride in the marriage ceremonies of many countries is regarded as a queen for the day and wears a crown; in others the place of the crown is taken by the bridal wreath.

The wreath or garland of flowers was, in Greek and Roman times, the diadem of Flora, goddess of flowers, and her marriage garland was usually of hawthorn blossom or verbena, which, as we have noted, are flowers which ward off evil powers. The Arabic bridal wreath was of orange blossom, a symbol of fertility. The wreath of flowers has a double symbolism in that it represents the flowers of virginity, but is also the funeral wreath which denotes dying to the old life and entering the new. Orange blossom, myrtle, olive and verbena are also symbols of fertility and were believed to impart creative powers. The apotropaic or protective properties of ornaments and talismanic adornments are of great importance on occasions when the person is the centre of attention to all around and therefore equally the focal point for the powers of good and evil in the world.

Sacrifices were often veiled and garlanded and the bride's veil and wreath share the symbolism of this custom since the bride sacrifices the old life of singleness and freedom and assumes the new state of unity and being bound by new ties. But the veil is also protection, concealing the head in which the life-power traditionally resides, and protecting the wearer from the public gaze and possible evil eye. Under the bride's veil her hair is 'put up', in the old days for the first time, since loose hair portrays freedom and bound hair the married status.

In the West, white, as a symbol of innocence, purity and virginity, is the bridal colour, though in Greece and China white was the colour of the spirit world and therefore of mourning. So the bridal dress is most usually of white, and, being a queen's dress, has a train which is carried by pages and the bride is followed by bridesmaids or ladies-in-waiting.

During the wedding ceremony the couple's hands are joined, signifying both union and pledged service; the right hand particularly pledges the life principle.

In many countries both bride and bridegroom assume the wedding ring. In some European lands the wedding ring is worn on the left hand at betrothal and then transferred to the right hand at marriage. After the ceremony, as the newly-wed pair leave the church or place of marriage, they are showered with confetti, or paper in the shape of flower petals. In olden days rice or grain was thrown. Round confetti represents grain, while the coloured petals take the place of flowers; both symbolize fertility. The old shoe tied to the going-away vehicle proclaims that the bride has been given into the possession of the bridegroom. The shoe can

stand for the person to whom it belongs, because in the days of
marriage by proxy the shoe was often sent in place of the person.
Finally, as we have seen, the bride must be carried over the
threshold of her new home in which she will rule.

Death Rites

All initiation ceremonies having the death-and-rebirth significance were also designed to take away the fear of death in
teaching the initiate that seeming death is only a transition to new
life. At physical death, the body, bereft of its life-giving force, the
breath, or soul, is placed once more in the shelter of the wood of
the tree, in the coffin, and then committed either to the earth or to
fire. Pine or cedar was often used as the wood of the coffin as
these woods were believed to preserve the body from corruption.
To be buried in the earth signifies the return to the womb of
Mother Earth to be born again into the next world. In some
civilizations the body was placed curled up in the foetal position
ready for rebirth. On the other hand, if the body is cremated,
being committed to the flames represents the rising of the soul to
the heavens, to a purified state and world. It is of interest to note
that countries which buried their dead often pictured their next
world as an underground place, such as the Greek Hades and the
Sheol of the Hebrews, while those which cremated the body
believed the soul to ascend with the flames to a sky-heaven. Few
people committed their dead to the waters, but the Celtic Paradise was across the waters, the Green Isle, as when King Arthur
set out across the waters with the Lady of the Lake. The Maori
Paradise is under the waters; Viking warriors were launched
seawards in burning boats.

But the most frequent idea of Paradise is that of an enclosed
garden or a perfect island cut off from the profane world by the
waters. Into that man is born again to start a new life once more.

12. Festivals

In many cases initiation ceremonies took place at the times of the great festivals. The origin of festivals lay in the idea of, and need for, man making himself practically and ritually one with the times, seasons and rhythms of nature. This was especially so in countries where the climate varied from one extreme to the other between the seasons. Various gods were associated with the sun and vegetation and it was obvious that their power died towards the end of the year, but regained life and vigour as the new year came and the days lengthened once more. The winter solstice was the dividing point between this death and rebirth and 25 December was the date most universally chosen for the Dying God's rebirth festival. He represented the ever-dying, ever-renewing cycle of nature; the youth of spring growing and maturing through the summer and dying with the autumn harvest, to remain dead until his rebirth at the turn of the year, which brought not only light and warmth to the soil and vegetation but, symbolically, also renewed light and life-wisdom to the mind of man.

As we have seen, all dying vegetation gods are slain, sometimes by being dismembered, in which case the god is brought back to life again by his female counterpart or devotees; or, more usually, he is killed on a tree. Osiris, Tammuz, Dionysos, Baal, Mithras, Attis, Balder, Woden/Odin are all dying gods and combine both the masculine and feminine principles; so, again, they are generally depicted as beautiful young men who never attain maturity, or as androgynous. As well as the characteristics already enumerated, Euripides says that the dying god is served by women and submits patiently to his fate, having incarnated to instruct mankind.

The Saturnalia

The Roman Saturnalia was the feast of Saturn, who was a god of agriculture, ruler of the Golden Age and Seventh Heaven, before he became associated with the winter solstice and, therefore, with dying, a symbolism which later developed into his portrayal as an old man with a sickle or scythe, the Reaper, Death, the Destroyer. The dead were supposed to return to the earth during the twelve nights of the Saturnalia that followed the birth of the Dying God. These were twelve days of chaos in which everything went into the melting pot and was turned upside down. The festival was governed by the Lord of Misrule, or the King of the Bean and the Queen of the Pea, a man or a couple who were chosen to reign for the period of the festival and to direct the merry-making, ceremonies and games. This time of chaos symbolized the re-entry into the primordial state that existed before the creation and the birth of the world and mankind. All the symbols of chaos were introduced into the festival, such as transvestism, 'fancy dress' and other disguises that all hide the normal nature and suggest confusion and loss of identity, hence signifying the primordial, undifferentiated oneness. As with carnivals, it also represented the Golden Age when all were equal. Evergreens were brought into the temples and houses, lamps were lit, presents exchanged, little images of men were made by the bakers and sweetmeats and candles were symbolic of plenty, light and good luck for the coming year. Masters and slaves exchanged places and slaves could wear hats and shoes that were normally symbols of freedom and the prerogative of the freeman and nobility. The King, or Lord of Misrule, took Saturn's place and licence reigned.

Sumeria also had a twelve-day festival of chaos connected with the worship of Marduk, the sun god who slew Tiamat, the monster of chaos and of the darkness of the underground and the waters. The twelve days were celebrated with mimes, merriment and the exchange of presents. Fires were lit, as sympathetic magic, to encourage the sun to gain strength. Evergreens were used as decorations; these trees, never becoming bare in winter, are a natural symbol of perpetual vitality, youth, vigour, deathlessness and immortality.

Christianity at first adopted 6 January, the last of the twelve days, when the mornings as well as the evenings begin to lengthen again, as the date for the celebration of Christ's birth and baptism; but later, in Europe, 25 December was substituted as it coincided with the Saturnalia—a time when the Romans were fully occupied with their own riotous carnival, which took their attention away from the persecuted Christians who were then free to celebrate their religious festival unmolested. Some five hundred years later the Church fixed the twelve days of Christmas definitely as running from 25 December to 6 January, the Epiphany.

Yuletide

It will be obvious that most of the Dying God ceremonies passed over into Christianity, but another strong influence in determining the customs of that festival came from the Gallic, Teutonic, Scandinavian and Celtic traditions of Yuletide. 'Yule' is said by some authorities to be derived from the Gallic 'gule', a wheel, probably representing the wheel of the turning sun and the revolution from the old to the new. As in ceremonies in other countries, yule also symbolized the return of chaos and the primeval darkness necessary before the new year can be born, a darkness and formlessness also symbolic of life in the womb before birth. It is the *regressus ad uterum* of myth and initiation rites. The cults of Tammuz, Attis, Dionysos, Woden/Odin and Thor are all apparent in the Yuletide celebrations. The first three of these gods were symbolized by the aniconic log, which was ritually burned at the end of the old year to signify the death of winter and the rising heat and power of the sun. Fire drives out darkness and cold and is a creative force; it burns the old and gives a fresh start to life, both vegetative and human, and the ashes, scattered on the earth, help to fertilize the new life that will emerge from the soil. The Yule-log was brought home ceremoniously, festooned with evergreens and bright ribbons, the most usual evergreen being ivy, the 'crown of Dionysos' and the 'plant of Osiris'. The log was of oak, the Cosmic Tree of the Druids.

The pine of Attis and the fir of Woden have continued to live as the Christmas Tree. Venerated generally in Teutonic cults, it was brought over to England at a late date by Prince Albert, who made it a feature of the Victorian royal Christmas, from which it passed into general custom. The pine of Attis, on which he was killed, was adopted into Christianity through the legend of St Boniface, who was reported to have stopped the sacrifice of a boy at the pagan oak ceremony and to have cut down the sacred oak. Seeing a small pine tree that had grown in the shadow of the oak, he then pointed to the evergreen as a symbol of life that never dies. With the tree, Christianity also took over the lights and luminous balls that represent the sun, moon and stars in the branches of the Cosmic Tree forming the canopy of the universe, but in addition they signified Christ as the Light of the World. Temples were also often lit by trees bearing lamps in their branches like fruits and flowers. Lights can also represent souls at festivals of the dead. In the Paradise Play (a mediaeval Mystery Play) the pine tree depicted Paradise and was hung with apples, a magic fruit, as a symbol of the Golden Age and of immortality.

Presents on trees had two different significances: the trees of Attis, Dionysos, Atargatis and Cybele, were hung with presents given by devotees as offerings to the divinities; but the fir tree of Woden bestowed gifts on all who venerated his sacred tree. For Christians, the gifts took on the significance of those brought to the infant Christ by the Magi. These gifts, in themselves, symbolized Christ's mission in life: gold for a king; frankincense for a priest and myrrh as sacrifice. The 'fairy' at the top of the tree was originally the angel who announced the birth of Christ to the shepherds. When a star takes the place of the fairy, it is that which led the Wise Men to Bethlehem.

With strong Teutonic-Nordic influences in Yuletide, there seems to be some connection between Father Christmas, Santa Claus, St Nicholas and Woden/Odin. The last appears at the beginning of the winter solstice and his date is 6 December, which coincides with that of St Nicholas, Bishop of Myra, about whom there were many legends of kindness and giving presents. He was said to have been devoted to children and delighted in giving them surprise gifts. Traditionally, as has been said, Santa Claus or Father Christmas must come down the chimney to bring his presents, since he is a magical person and therefore must not touch the earth. The chimney has its special significance as being an opening to the sky and heavenly powers.

Various other saints are associated with December festivals of light. In Sweden St Lucia, whose day is the 13th, is represented by the oldest girl in the family. She wears a crown of evergreen and lighted candles, depicting the end of winter darkness and the coming of light in the lengthening days and melting of the ice. She wakes the family that day and sings:

> Now St Lucia's day has come
> Darkness cannot linger,
> Cold, soon banished by the sun,
> Lifts his icy finger.

In Holland, St Nicholas comes by ship from Spain, bringing presents. Switzerland also has St Nicholas and French children put out their sabots in the hearth to be filled with his gifts.

The oak and the mistletoe were sacred to the Druids as the masculine and feminine powers in nature, mistletoe being the Golden Bough of the Druids. The oak provided the Yule Log and mistletoe was hung from the ceiling at the festival. Growing out of the oak, mistletoe was taken as representing the life-force or essence of the oak tree and was therefore a divine substance. It was believed that it grew as a result of the branch being struck by lightning. This gave it special spiritual qualities, as anything or anyone struck by lightning is favoured of the gods. Because of its spiritual qualities and magical nature, mistletoe must never touch the ground but is always suspended in mid-air. When the Druids cut the mistletoe, with a golden sickle, it was caught in white sheets to prevent it falling to the ground. Being itself neither tree nor shrub, it is that which is neither one thing nor the other, which, by analogy, places it in the realm of freedom from limitations. Thus anyone standing under the mistletoe is free from normal restrictions and has entered the world of chaos in which anything can happen; but in such a situation the person is also free from protection. This, and the fact that mistletoe is also a love symbol, gave rise to kissing under the mistletoe. When the Yuletide festival is over, the mistletoe is sometimes burned at Twelfth Night, or kept until Shrove Tuesday, another coming-of-light festival, when it is burned to light the flame that cooks the pancakes. Mistletoe is also associated with the Norse Balder, or Baldur, a dying god, in the well-known myth in which mistletoe caused his death.

The dying god Dionysos has ivy as his sacred plant as well as the vine. He is depicted crowned with ivy and his cup is the 'ivy cup'; his thyrsus has ivy wound round it and ivy was wound round the log that represented him. The revelry associated with his worship gave ivy the dual significance of immortality and eternal life as an evergreen, and revelry was always connected with his orgies. Ivy was also sacred to the Phrygian Attis and the Egyptian Osiris. The ivy-leaf was also phallic, which explains its discrete use on nude male statues. The fig leaf has the same import.

Holly was sacred to Saturn and was one of the evergreens used to deck his temples at the Saturnalia. It was also an attribute of the sun gods and signifies joy, goodwill, health and happiness. Christianity took it over as a symbol of the crucifixion. Its wood is sometimes taken as the tree of the cross (as are also the oak and the aspen) and its spikes are the crown of thorns and the passion, with the berries as the blood of Christ. The robin joins the holly in this symbolism, its red breast representing the blood of the cross, symbols which live on in our Christmas cards. Cards are, however, a modern innovation and have no symbolic significance, except as tokens of the ancient custom of exchange of presents.

In earlier times farm animals were killed off at the onset of winter when fodder became scarce. The meat was salted, dried or preserved for use during the winter months. The chief meat was pork, and many old kitchens in farm and country houses still have the large hooks in the ceilings from which the legs of ham and flitches of bacon hung. With pork as the chief winter meat, it is not surprising that the boar's head was the central dish at the Yuletide festival, the head being symbolic of the seat of power and vitality. The boar's head was brought in with great ceremony and had sprigs of rosemary, an evergreen and also a funerary plant, in its ears and an apple in its mouth. But apart from its being a winter meat, the boar, a symbol of fertility, procreation, protection, courage and hospitality, was sacred to Woden/Odin and Frey, Norse fertility deities, and was sacrificed to them at Yule.

Other foods eaten at Yuletide are plum puddings and mince pies. The plum pudding started as a fruit and spice porridge and mince pies were originally made of minced meat, usually mutton. For the Christian Christmas, the mince pie cases were shaped like a cradle to represent the manger of the infant Jesus. A mince pie was eaten on each of the twelve days of Christmas, to bring good luck to each of the twelve months of the year to come. Incidentally, these twelve days were supposed to show the pattern of the weather to come in the following months. The Christmas goose is, as we have seen, a solar bird. Eaten at Michaelmas and Christmas, it represents first the waning then the growing power of the sun. The turkey, to which reference has already been made, is a comparative late-comer to Christmas festivities and was brought over from America.

The 'wassail' was a hot, spiced ale, later changed to punch. Healths (*was haile*) were drunk in it and people went from house to house carousing and health-drinking, as in the carol 'Here we come a-wassailing'. In regions where cider was drunk it held the symbolic magic of the Celtic apple, the fruit of the Silver Bough.

The miming, dancing and mumming of the ancient Sumerians during the twelve days of merrymaking and time of chaos have passed on down the ages. In mediaeval times in Europe mumming, with its masks and transvestism, continued the tradition, and boys and girls in towns and villages went from house to house to give the traditional plays, which were always on the theme of the triumph of light over darkness and hence of good over evil. St George's defeat of the dragon was a typical subject, or the Old Year was killed either in the play or a symbolic dance. The carols of Christianity were originally ring, or round, dances, performed to a sung tune, round a crib, either in a church or in the home. Most carols perpetuated the dying god symbols of the star, virgin birth, wise men and the God-King-Sacrifice. Now only the vestigial remains of these ceremonies continue in our non-dancing carols, while the play, although still performed in some places, has largely degenerated into the pantomime, in which the transformation scene unwittingly still depicts the old chaos and rebirth symbols, though the fairy tales, on which pantomimes are based, were originally highly symbolic. Cinderella, for example, is the journey of the soul from the state of heavenly bliss (the story should start with Ella, who was perfectly happy in her home until her mother died and her father married again, and her ugly sisters, symbolic of the evils of this world, reduced her to the drudge Cinder-ella) down to the trials and tribulations of earthly incarnation, in which she is helped or hindered by good and bad forces until she wins through to perfection and attains unity.

New Year and Easter

After the Christmas festival comes the New Year which, in the West, begins in January, though the old Celtic year started with Samhain, or Samhuinn, the Festival of the Dead, which marked the beginning of winter and the breakdown between the two worlds. This was the origin of the Hallowe'en ceremonies at the beginning of November, representing chaos and the return of the dead—a time adopted by Christianity as the Feast of All Souls and All Saints.

The month of January takes its name from the Roman Janus, god of keys and doors, both of which are symbols of the power of opening and closing. He is depicted as holding a key in his left hand and a staff in his right. He is two-faced which not only suggests the dual role of opening and closing, binding and loosing, but also the two natures of man, which can be in conflict with each other, until he becomes integrated and achieves mental and spiritual wholeness. Silver and gold keys also signify temporal and spiritual power. Janus controls the two doors of *Janua inferni* (the 'door of men') which occurs in the sign of Cancer when the sun starts on its downward path, and *Janua coeli* (the 'door of the gods'), in Capricorn, when the New Year comes and the sun begins to gain power. The latter leads heavenwards, the former leads to the lower regions. The heavenwards door opens up new possibilities and brings rebirth, hence the making of New Year resolutions.

Formerly, eggs, which were not eaten during Lent, became the Easter food; but the Easter Egg and the Easter Hare, Rabbit or 'Bunny', are all pre-Christian symbols of fertility, rebirth and resurrection and the resurgence of life at the vernal equinox. Easter is a lunar festival of the first full moon after the equinox and probably took its name from Eastre, or Ostara, Teutonic goddess of spring and the dawn. The hare was her sacred animal and was sacrificed to her. It was the hare that laid the Easter Egg, round which all sorts of customs, too numerous to detail, have arisen.

In Christianity the Paschal or Easter Candle, which is made of pure wax with grains of incense in the shape of nails, represents the body of God Incarnate bringing the light of heaven to the world and the nails are, of course, those of the crucifixion. The candle is burned during the forty days from Easter to Ascension and symbolizes Christ's presence with the Disciples for the forty days after the resurrection. Extinguished on Ascension Day, it denotes the removal of Christ from the earth. It also depicts the light of the risen Christ, as well as the pillar of fire which guided the Israelites for forty years.

Spring Festivals
Spring and May Day festivals, which were often accompanied by orgies, typified the marriage of the Sun God, or Sky Father, with the Earth Mother, the union necessary to give birth to the forces of nature. The orgies were to encourage those powers by sympathetic magic and imitative fertility, a practice which, in the light of modern research into plant responses and sensitivity, now appears to have had some foundation other than superstition and magic. The maypole was one of the symbols of fertility, both in its structure and the dance round it. Originally it was the sacred pine of Attis and was taken in procession, followed by men, women and children, to the temple of Cybele, consort of Attis, and was set up there. Dances were held round it. The ceremony passed later into

the Roman Hilaria, a Spring festival. The pole of the maypole is also the axis round which the earth revolves. In its fertility symbolism it is phallic, while the discus at the top of the pole is the feminine principle, the two together naturally making for fertility. The seven coloured ribbons hanging from the pole were thought to represent the bands of wool that bound Attis to the tree. They are also the colours of the rainbow, a symbol of transformation, transfiguration and the meeting of heaven and earth, forming a bridge between the realms of the Sky God and Earth Mother.

Autumn Festivals

After the growth of the summer comes the maturity of autumn, after which life, having reached its peak, declines and begins to die at harvest time. The safe conclusion of the harvesting of the crops has always been a time for rejoicing in agricultural communities and the Harvest Home began with the ceremonial bringing in of the last sheaf of corn in triumph. This was followed by merrymaking and feasting. There has always been a particular significance attached to the last remnant, in which power was believed to be concentrated; the last sheaf of corn, the seeds of plants, the scrapings of the dough of the Yuletide cake, are all charged with a special potency. The Corn Dolly, made at harvest time, represents not only the Corn Goddess but also the seed, the form and potential growth of the future harvest. Lammas, the harvest-time festival at the beginning of August, means 'loaf-mass', the feast of the first fruits, to celebrate and give thanks for the safe gathering of the harvest. The loaves were often baked in the shape of a sheaf of corn, a custom still seen in churches in the produce displayed at Harvest Festivals.

13. Games and Play

Dancing and play have always been associated with festivals in the rhythmic energy of the cosmos, the rhythm of the universe. They also project the symbol into movement. Play is the method by which the powers of the universe, or the Divinity, create and express themselves in manifestation and we naturally speak of the 'play' of these forces. It is also an expression of the exuberant energy of the Creator. Again, we speak of the 'play' of the sunlight, which fertilizes and illuminates, and there is the interplay of the male-female powers, the opposing but complementary forces. Play also signifies the part that man acts out on the stage of life. This play in the manifest world is most adequately expressed in Hinduism and Tantric Buddhism in the play of the creative deity in the Dance of Siva in creating the world of phenomena, of *maya* or illusion. It is interesting to note here that the word 'illusion' is derived from the Latin to play a game.

All traditional play and dancing is governed by rules. In games there are winning or losing moves, actions and choices that influence the outcome of the game and which are irreversible once taken. In dancing, the rhythmic movement transforms space into time, in imitation of the divine play, and reinforces its strength in emotion and activity.

Dances
Round dances are solar in significance and follow the sun's movement in the heavens, while sword and morris dances developed from sympathetic magic, helping the sun on its rounds. With this also goes the fertility element. Dancing round an object, or the ceremony of 'beating the bounds', or any other ritual involving circumlocution, encloses that which is within the circle in a magic protective space, which also strengthens the object. In

the monotheistic religions, the round dance depicts angels round the throne of God.

Chain dances represent the linking of male and female, heaven and earth. Thread and rope dances recall the thread of Ariadne, which represents the secret knowledge of the way in and out of the maze of life and the way to the centre. Troy, or labyrinth dances, also called miz-maze, Julian's Bower and Shepherd's Race, are of such antiquity that their origins are lost, but obviously they, too, gave protection and strength to the object at the centre. If a maiden or some special object were placed at the centre, the dancing of the maze took on the symbolism of a quest and the central figure was the goal. Troy Towns or Troy dances could be marked by enclosing banks, hedges and walls, or simply by grass paths or the pattern on a church floor, such as that in the cathedral at Chartres. The significance of this tracing of the pattern of the labyrinth has variously been suggested as the return to Paradise, finding the Centre, or the trials, temptations and difficulties that beset mankind in the world and that must be solved and overcome in the passage of life from birth to death, from the profane world to the sacred. It is a symbol of both exclusion and difficulty and of entering and finding.

Games

Ball games are symbolic of the power of the gods in hurling globes, stars and meteorites across the skies. The ball can also represent either the sun or the moon and ball games have been associated with both solar and lunar festivals.

Toys are equated with childhood and innocence, but also with temptation and distracting the mind from the more serious aspects of life and leading it to dissipation and frivolities. Some individual toys have a significance of their own: Bastius says that the spinning top has the same symbolism as the pine cone, a spiral whorl and a vortex—that is to say, the great generative forces. Christianity added a symbolism to the whipping top, played with during Lent, as representing the scourging of Christ. Some say the lashing of a hoop has the same significance.

The drum is an attribute of all Thunder Gods: it typifies primordial sound and speech (the drum 'speaks') and is revelation of truth. In Africa it represents the heart and magic power. For Buddhism it is the Voice of the Law, 'the drum of the immortal in the darkness of the world', which wakens the ignorant and slothful. In Shinto temples the drum calls people to prayer. The

Shaman's drum is symbolically made from the Cosmic Tree and has magic powers in calling up spirits. In Taoism the drum is the Voice of Heaven and is the emblem of the Immortal Chang Kuo-lao. Hinduism comes nearer to the thunder god symbolism in giving the drum to Siva and Kali as destroyers. In Greece it was equated with orgies; it also has a place in tribal sexual and war dances.

Any flying indicates aspiration, transcendence and the release of the spirit from the limitations of the body; also the passage from one plane to another. Kites thus take part in this symbolism and, in the East, were used at festivals and on some ritual occasions, such as the Dragon Festival. They were made in the most elaborate forms of dragons, birds and other symbolic creatures.

The trumpet has always been associated with occasions of pomp and ceremony, fame and glory. It heralds the arrival of royalty and heroes; it can also call to war.

Swinging and rocking and see-saws are connected with fertility rites, but also symbolize life's vicissitudes as well as the rhythms of the universe.

Chess

So ancient is the game of chess that nothing is known of its origins, except that they were eastern. It has been suggested that it developed from nomads marking out a limited area on the ground and playing games with moving pebbles, a sort of Fox and Geese. A legend attributes its invention to a philosopher-mathematician at the court of an Indian king who, like Alexander the Great, had no more worlds to conquer and was becoming bored and restive. The battle of chess, which could be played endlessly, was the answer to the king's problems. The legend goes on to say that the king was so pleased that he promised the philosopher-inventor anything he might ask. The reply was that he would like one grain of rice for the first square, two for the second, and so on, squaring the number up to the sixty-four squares. The king thought this an unduly modest request and ordered the rice to be put up in sacks; but after the sum had at last been calculated it was reported to the king that there was not that much grain in the whole of his kingdom. He then had to apologize to the philosopher, who laughed and said he did not want the rice but was glad to have taught the king not to make rash promises.

Chess is known as the royal game of life and symbolizes the conflict between the two spiritual powers of light and darkness, the *devas* and the *asuras*, angels and demons, who are perpetually struggling for dominion over the world. The chequer board represents all known dualities and complementaries in the world of manifestation: negative and positive, night and day, time and space, sun and moon, and so on endlessly. The sixty-four squares are those of the mandala of Siva and are based on the four-fold symbolism of the 8 × 8, which is the basic form of a temple, city or sacred monument, constructed on traditional lines. It symbolizes all the possibilities in the universe and in man and so implies perfection. There is also an Indian circular chess-board which signifies infinity and the Round of Birth and Death. Each game is an epoch and putting away the pieces is equated with a period of non-manifestation, a 'night of Brahma'. The movement of the pieces comprises all possibilities in the world of form, and, while the choice of movement is free, the act of moving sets in train an inescapable series of results, for which the mover is responsible, as in the laws of *karma*; so both free-will and determination, or destiny, are involved.

Each piece on the board represents some function, ability, quality or thing existing in the world. The King is the sun, the heart and the forces of law and order. He can only move one square at a time because he is limited by law in manifestation. Beside him is the Queen, or Vizier, or Councillor, who is the moon, the spirit, the Mover at Will, who can make any move in any direction except the Knight's. The Elephant, or Bishop, represents the rulers of things spiritual and the move is based on the triangle: moving on white squares denotes the positive and intellectual path, while black squares are the negative, emotional and devotional way on the spiritual quest. The diagonal movement is ruled by Jupiter and typifies the feminine and existential. The Rook, Castle, or Chariot, signifies the rulers of this world, temporal power, and the move is based on the square which symbolizes the earth and axial movement, cutting across differences of colours. It is ruled by Saturn and is the virile and masculine. The straight move is also consistent with the movement of the chariot. The Rook is also said to be the dreaded Roc of fable. The Knight, with his two-way move, is involved in both the intellectual and devotional path, since he represents the initiate, but lacks, as yet, the power of the Spirit. His move is also equated with the jump of intuition and it has been suggested that the Knight has, in the West, military and chivalric associations with initiatory orders, such as the Templars, and that he is the 'wanderer' or knight errant. He is ruled by Mars, god of war. Pawns are ordinary people, attempting to win their way through life, across the board, through the seven grades of initiation, to reach the eighth square, the realm of the spiritual, of completion, of Paradise Regained, the final goal of the initiate. To attain to the eighth square converts the pawn into a Queen and it becomes a Mover at Will, one who has achieved enlightenment. Pawns are both male and female, ruled by Mercury and Venus, the pair of lovers.

14. Numbers

In many ancient traditions number was considered to be a fundamental principle. All things originated from number and it was responsible for the harmony of the universe. Numbers were not merely a question of quantity but had an important symbolic quality; that is to say, they are both quantitive and qualitive. According to Pythagoras, whose system of philosophy and cosmology was based on numbers, 'Everything is disposed according to numbers.' In Hindu and Babylonian cultures, numbers are also the basis of the cosmos.

There is striking agreement in all ages and traditions on certain number symbolism. Starting with zero, we have nothingness, the non-existent, that which is yet unmanifest and has neither quality nor quantity. It is the Void, the Absolute, the ultimate mystery. It is also the perfect form, which, as the Void, is the originator and container of all. It takes on the full symbolism of the circle. It is the Cosmic Egg from which all is born, it is the nothingness of death, but also the ultimate perfection of the Androgyne. In Qabalism the Void is the Ain, the incomprehensible, that which is beyond being. This parallels the Taoist Void, the Tao and the Pythagorean universal totality.

The One and the Duad
From the Void comes the First Mover, the Creator, the One, and in creation there is the entry into the world of phenomena. In its most elementary form, the One is the 'I' as distinct from others, while in philosophy and metaphysics its symbolism is highly complex. Though it is the indivisible, isolation, it is yet the germinal and the principle which gives rise to duality and from thence to multiplicity. As Taoism puts it: 'Tao begets One, One begets Two, Two begets Three and Three begets all things.' The

One, the Monad, gives rise to the Two, the Duad, but both Monad and Duad are principles rather than numbers. The Duad is the first 'break away' and the original unity is lost. Relativity, dependence, otherness, and the possibility of conflict enters, so that the Duad also represents deviation from the first perfection and hence sin, the transitory and the corruptible. The First Cause is perfection. Evil is thus a falling away from the Good into diversity. From the Duad arise all the opposites in nature. In Alchemy these opposites are at first antagonistic, but through the Great Work are ultimately restored to unity in the Androgyne. In Buddhism the opposites are Wisdom and Method, the Blind and the Lame, who unite to see the Way and walk in it, while Tantric Buddhism employs the sex symbolism of male and female: the male Method applies the female Wisdom in practice, the initial vision of knowing and truth.

Taoism divides all numbers into *yin* and *yang*. The even numbers are *yin* and weaker because they lack a centre, while odd numbers are *yang* and strong because if divided the centre remains. This is echoed by Plato who said that two is a digit without meaning since it implies relationship, which must introduce a third factor. In Taoism and Tantric Buddhism it is accepted that mankind is tremendously involved in the dualities and that life must bring struggle; but if either *yang* or *yin*, god or goddess, male or female, prevails over the other the natural balance is lost and this inevitably upsets the symmetry and harmony of the physical, mental and spiritual life. Neither of the dualities must be over-developed or repressed, or violent reaction and malaise result. Both must be accepted as an essential element in the work of transformation on the way to enlightenment or realization.

Three

From the Duad develops the plural (that is, anything outside a pair), the first then being three. As Aristotle said: 'Of two things men say "both", but not "all" ... three is the first number to which the term "all" has been appropriated.' The number three has an accumulative effect. Once or twice may be a coincidence, but three times becomes something in the nature of a law. To impress a thing it is repeated three times: 'One, two, three—go'; 'For the third and last time'; 'Going, going, gone!'; 'Thrice-noble Lord'; 'Thrice happy isles', and so on. 'Having unity in the midst' and being indivisible, three is also incorruptible, hence its power

Three

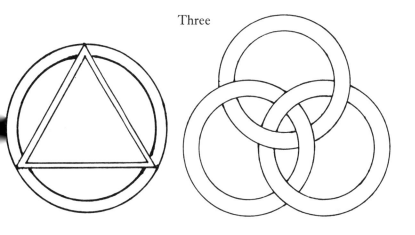

Trinity symbols

Triquetra

and good luck. Three also implies the heavens, the consummate power, such as 'Trismagistus', the thrice great. The threes are endless: three tries, three wishes, the three princes, princesses, fairies, witches of folklore and fairy tale, the three Golden Apples of Atalanta, the three Fates, and, carried over into Christianity, the three Magi and their three gifts, three figures of the trans-formation, three temptations, Peter's three denials, three days of Christ's death before the resurrection and three appearances after it. Three also introduces the all-embracing character of the Godhead, the Trinity, which in turn is reflected in the human family—Father, Mother, Child. It is also birth, life, death; past, present, future.

There are the great Trinities of the various religions; in Egypt, Osiris, Isis and Horus, the Babylonian Sin, Shamash, Ishtar, the Scandinavian Odin, Thor, Frey, etc., of which the Gilgamish Epic says: 'Two thirds of him is God, and one third of him is man.' This applied to the Christian Trinity over two thousand years later. The pre-eminent symbol of the number three is the triangle. Plato said that surface is composed of triangles, as it is the first plane figure.

Four, Five and Six

As three is the most fundamental representation of surface, four produces the first solid. Four is the symbol of the earth, with its four cardinal points, four elements, four winds, four seasons and the four quarters of the moon dividing the months into four weeks. It is represented by the square, the cross and the cube, all symbols of solidity and completeness but also of the static as opposed to the dynamism of the circular symbols. Four is also the number of the body with its two hands and two feet, but with the inclusion of the head as an extremity the number of man then becomes five, the pentacle.

Five is the primitive counting number with the five fingers doubling to ten and then including the toes to make twenty, in all making a convenient round number for reckoning—the primitive decimal system. There are also five senses and five primary colours. It is regarded as a circular number since it reproduces itself in its last digit when raised to its powers. The Pentacle, being endless, also shares the symbolism of the circle. It is often represented by the five-petalled rose or lily.

Plato calls six 'the most productive of all numbers' as it is the first perfect number (that is $1 + 2 + 3 = 6$) and it is therefore a number of harmony and balance, implying beauty, health and good luck. The six-pointed star, which is the interlacing of the two triangles, is the upward-pointing male and fire with the downward-pointing female and water symbols; it also, by extension, depicts the union of opposites and the hermaphrodite.

Seven and Eight

With three as the number of the heavens and four as the earth, the two together comprise completeness, totality. Seven is also made up of the first odd number with the first even number and so is the first to contain both the spiritual and the temporal. It is thus the number of the universe and of the whole man. As the cosmic number there are seven heavens, seven hells, seven major planets, lunar divisions of the rainbow, days of the week and ages of man. In the Bible, in both the Old and New Testaments, the influence of seven is constant. As there are seven heavens and hells, so the good and bad spirits number seven. Seven devils are cast out of possessed people. This baleful aspect of seven goes back to the Babylonian influence on Judaism in the Captivity, and hence later on Christianity. The Babylonian Ziggurat, a temple constructed in the form of the Cosmic Mountain, had seven steps of ascent to heaven, but the lunar week brought the seventh day into opposition with the sun and so made it a day of darkness and evil. It was unlucky to undertake anything on the seventh day or any multiple of seven. This is probably the origin of the seventh day being a day of rest, any activity then being dangerous. Seven appears as a sacred number in most religions. The Brahmanas give seven Gods before the Flood and seven wise men saved from it. It is also an important number spiritually in Pythagoreanism. Seven days form the period of fasting and penitence, so after that comes the eighth day which brings good and plenty again.

The Jubilee is derived from this seven-to-eight symbolism. After the 7×7 cycle of years comes the fiftieth, a Great Year, a time of rejoicing and a fresh start. (This is the basis of the timing of the Olympic Games every four years, or fifty lunations.)

As we have seen from the chess board, the pawn tries to cross the seven squares to reach the eighth in order to achieve initiation and become a Mover at Will. The eighth degree is thus the spiritual goal of the initiate who passes through the seven stages, or heavens. This is Paradise Regained, regeneration and rebirth. The baptismal font in churches is often octagonal in shape, symbolizing this initiatory power of regeneration. The octagon, often used in the domes of temples or cathedrals, represents not only the perfection of the number but is also the beginning of the squaring of the circle, and hence the union of the powers of heaven and earth.

Nine and Ten
Composed of the multiplication of the all-powerful number three, nine is a perfect number. It is a 'whole' number and so is also completion and fulfilment. It is also an angelic number and there are triple-triads of angels. Enneads occur in most traditions but in the North, in Celtic and Scandinavian lands, it is especially notable how the number nine dominates. It is extremely powerful in magic, as is seen in *Macbeth*: 'Thrice to thine and thrice to mine, and three again to make it nine.' Odin hung for nine days on the tree; the northern Persephone, Skeldi, Goddess of Snow, lives in her mountains for three months, then returns to her husband for nine months. Nine dominates the Celtic Beltane fire rites, which are attended by eighty-one men, nine at a time. In Chinese symbolism nine is the most peaceful and luckiest of all numbers. As the 3 × 3 it is the great celestial number. It also represents the eight directions of space with nine as the all-important centre.

Based on the two hands, ten is completeness and, as it contains all the other numbers, it is also all possibilities. It is the number of law and order and dominion and therefore of divinity. Ten is also the number of return and many of the legendary voyagers, such as Odysseus, return in the tenth year, thus conforming to the symbolism of ten as the return to the origins, to unity.

After ten, all numbers start again. The higher ranges of the number, a hundred and a thousand, are the basis of Hindu cosmology. In China the 'Ten Thousand Things' means not only the uncountable but also the whole of manifestation. In Judaism ten plays a significant part, especially in Solomon's Temple, where there were ten loaves, tables, candlesticks and cherubim, with ten Levites to minister before the Ark Of the Lord. The Ten Commandments reflect the divine number and support. The ten aeons of Gnosticism become the Sephiroth of Qabalism, emanating from the Pleroma.

Other Numbers
Eleven, going beyond the law of ten, becomes a number of excess and therefore of sin. But twelve is of considerable importance in

many religions and cults. It is the number of the Zodiac and the months of the year, of which six are female and six male, and there are the twelve hours of the day and night. The gods and goddesses of Olympus numbered twelve. The Roman law had twelve tablets, while the twelve days of chaos at the end of the old year and beginning of the new were, as we have seen, celebrated in civilizations and ages from the Babylonian, to the Roman, to the Celtic and to modern times. Twelve is also a typical number of disciples. Mithras had that number of followers, as had Christ in the New Testament. There were the Twelve Tribes of Israel in the Old Testament and Islam has the twelve descendants of Ali, the Imams.

In Christian countries, thirteen is regarded as unlucky since there were the twelve Disciples and Christ seated at the table at the Last Supper and the thirteenth, the first to rise from the table, was the traitor Judas Iscariot. Thirteen is also the number of a witches' coven, but in Mayan and Aztec times it was the number of the heavens and the gods and was important in the calendar. It was also the great divination number.

Following twenty as the digital reckoning of the whole man, forty becomes the next significant figure, probably deriving from the disappearance for forty days of the Pliades in the Babylonian calendar, which presaged the time of storms, floods and danger. When the Pliades returned to the heavens there was rejoicing and feasting and forty reeds were burned to symbolize the passing of the period of the evil power. The Romans had a forty-day duration of quarantine for ships. Many temples were built with forty pillars. In Judaism there are the forty days of the Flood, and there are the forty days in Christianity when Christ was in the wilderness and which are still kept as the forty days of Lent. Moses was forty days on Sinai and there are various other examples in the Old Testament. Forty thus becomes a 'fated' time, one of trial and initiation but then of return and reconciliation.

The next symbolic number after fifty, the Great Year, is sixty, the number of time in seconds and minutes. It is a cyclic number, being a round three score. It has particular importance in China as the 'cycle of sixty', known in the West as a 'cycle of Cathay'. After that, seventy occurs in Hebrew symbolism as the 'three score years and ten' of man's allotted span.

For Plato number is the archetype of the Absolute: 'There is a relation of numbers which cannot possibly be impaired or altered, nor can any nature by violence prevent the number which comes after one from being the double of one . . . it is not in any man's power to determine at his pleasure that 3×3 are not nine, or are not a triple of three.' The Pythagoreans, heirs to the Babylonian system, maintained that a knowledge of numbers was equivalent to a knowledge of the workings of God and the cosmos. Everything was influenced and conducted by numbers.

15. The Body and its Clothes

The body is, obviously, equated with the material world and earthly life, but the 'new body', spoken of in initiatory and sacramental rites, is regarded as a death to the earthly, unregenerate man and a birth into a new state of spiritual regeneration and powers. However, the earthly body carries a wider symbolism than this in its various members, the two most important of which are the head and the heart.

The Head and the Heart

The head is regarded as the chief seat of the life-force. It denotes mind, control, wisdom, the soul and its powers. But the head, as well as being the seat of intelligence, is also the place where folly dwells. This dual role of the head is demonstrated in ceremonies and rites of honour and dishonour. The crown of the sovereign, of glory, the wreath of the victor, are all placed on the head, but so are the fool's cap, the dunce's cap, 'coals of fire' of reproach and the ashes of mourning and penitence. The origin of 'busts' of famous people lies in the making of images of the heads that were placed on tombs to represent the life-force or genius of the person.

As we have seen, the heads of animals, sacrificed or hunted, such as the boar, horse or bull, were regarded as containing the vital power and were hung up ceremoniously, or carried in ritual procession, or eaten at ritual festivals. Tribal head- or scalp-hunters valued the head of the enemy as holding the life-force of both the head and the hair, which, when captured, transferred their powers to the victor and possessor.

Gestures involving the head continue this symbolism: to bow the head is to lower the life-force before another, either in honour, assent, shame or submission. Nodding the head is a pledge of this power, while shaking it in the opposite direction denotes negation and refusal. All covering of the head, as in wearing hats, caps, veils or garlands, hides and protects the inner life of the head; but the veil can also depict secrecy, hidden knowledge and the inscrutable.

In religious iconography, two-headed gods, such as Janus, signify past and present, beginning and end, solar and lunar powers, and so on. The Dioscuri, with heads looking upwards and downwards, portray day and night and the sun in the upper and lower hemispheres. Triple-headed gods represent the three realms of past, present and future; the three phases of the moon, and the rising, noontide and setting sun. Serapis, Hecate and Cernunnos are sometimes so depicted. Divinities with multiple heads or faces signify the All-seeing. They also show the different aspects, exploits and functions of the deity, or they can combine various gods. Some can also represent elemental powers, cycles and seasons.

The heart is also a centre of being, both physical and spiritual; but it symbolizes the wisdom of the feelings and emotions as contrasted with the reasoning intelligence of the head. The heart contains the life-blood, and holds the powers of love, charity and compassion. It is also the 'secret place', and, although it is associated with the emotions rather than with reason, it is said to have 'reasons that the reason knows not of'. The chief symbol of the heart is the sun, the centre of the universe, and the rayed sun and the radiant or flaming heart depict the centre of the macro-cosmos and microcosmos. The heart is also portrayed by the downard-pointing triangle. The cave, as secrecy, is another of its symbols. In the East, the heart is also depicted by the lotus. The diamond heart of Buddhism stands for purity and indestructibil-ity—that which nothing can 'cut' or disturb. The heart-sacrifice of the Aztecs signified the liberating of the life-force, the seed of life, to germinate and flower again. Blood, as the life-principle, is equated with rejuvenating force and strength and sometimes typifies the soul. Blood and water are used in Chinese symbolism as the *yang* and *yin* principles, while in Christianity they represent the life of the body and the life of the spirit. Blood and wine are almost universally interchangeable symbols.

The Hand
Aristotle said that the hand is 'the tool of tools'. Its use certainly gives man advantage in adaptability and possibilities when com-

pared with most other animals. The hand can both attract and repel, grasp or push away, and is therefore associated with both these powers. It can also be extended in protection, blessing and providence. The Great Hand depicts supreme power, the Deity. In religious art the Hand of God is not only protection but transmits the power of the Spirit. There are endless symbolic attitudes and gestures of the hands and, in Hinduism and Buddhism, there is a complete language of manual expression of divine power and human response known as *mudra*. The hand is one of the most expressive members of the body. As Quintillian said: 'The hands may almost be said to speak. Do we not use them to demand, promise, summon, dismiss, threaten, supplicate, express aversion or fear, question and deny? Do we not use them to indicate joy, sorrow, hesitation, confession, penitence, measure, quantity, number and time? Have they not the power to excite and prohibit, to express approval, wonder, shame?'

Extending and clasping hands naturally implies friendliness. The bare hand, without a weapon in it, obviously meant that the approach was not hostile but suggested welcome. An outstretched hand is also blessing and protection and to place one's hand in another's is to render it harmless and therefore to give a pledge of friendship and service. Shaking hands forms a cross, or ankh, of covenant. Clasping hands also signifies union, allegiance, or mystic marriage. Folded hands are equated with repose, restfulness and immobility, while hands folded across the breast are a gesture of submission and servitude. Open hands ('open handed') are bounty, liberality, hospitality and justice; the closed hand is the reverse ('close fisted'), the secretive; while the clenched fist is aggression, hostility and provocation. Raised hands typify worship, prayer, salutation or surrender and hence an admission of weakness, but they also open the person to receiving power from on high. When the right hand is held up alone it is a gesture of blessing and pledges the life-principle. Hands placed together take on an attitude of prayer, implying defencelessness, inferiority, the bearing of a subject before a greater power, but also allegiance. This is also the Eastern and Buddhist form of salutation, and, apart from its religious significance, implies the courtesy of regarding the other person as superior.

Washing hands ritually is a token of innocence, purity, repudiation of guilt, just as Pontius Pilate washed his hands of responsibility for the condemnation and death of Christ. It also cleanses ritually before participating in religious ceremonies. The laying-on of hands in rites transmits power, grace or healing. In the West the right hand is the 'hand of power' and is the one that is offered in greeting or blessing, while the left hand represents the passive, receptive aspect. But in China, while the right hand was *yang* and strength, the left hand, the *yin*, was the hand of honour, since the right is the sword hand and thus associated with war, violence and destruction. This was reversed in the time of war, when the *yang* became the military hand of honour. In traditional China, the hand was not extended in greeting, for although clasped hands depicted friendliness and greeting or allegiance, concealing the hands denoted deference and respect, so hands were hidden in the broad cuffs of the sleeves, while those greeting each other bowed.

In art, a hand appearing from the clouds portrays the presence, power and might of God. This is especially so in Christian iconography. In Islam the Hand of Fatima represents the Hand of God, with the thumb as the Prophet and the fingers as his four companions. The five fingers are also the five fundamental dogmas and the five pillars of the Islamic religion. The Votive Hand of Sabazios, found in Sumero-Semitic and Greek art, is suggested as the helping hand of God, or the Earth Mother, as bounteous giver and protector; or it may have been merely talismanic since it was accompanied by other symbols on the palm and fingers, such as the snake, cross, cone, crescent, lizard and insects.

One was told as a child that it is rude to point; but pointing was worse than rude in origin since the pointing finger was not only an insult but could contain a direct magic power against the person. Magicians, even today in entertainments, point the finger at the object concerned in any magic command.

When the hand is raised in blessing with three fingers, these represent the Trinity. Two fingers depict help and strength and were particularly associated with Osiris and Horus, the first finger being divine justice and the second the Spirit, the Mediator. A finger across the mouth is a symbol of silence or warning; it is a characteristic of the Infant Horus.

The thumb depicts power and transmission of that power, hence being 'under the thumb'. Raised upwards it is beneficent power; downwards it is the reverse, ill-luck and death. This symbolism was used in the Roman arenas either to spare or condemn the life of a gladiator.

Arms upraised denote supplication, prayer or surrender, but

the arms also signify protection, power and help. The many-armed gods and goddesses of Hinduism and Buddhism portray unlimited compassionate aid and they often carry various symbols of the different powers and operation of divine power in the universe.

The Foot

The chief agent of movement is the foot which thus symbolizes freedom to come and go, or willing service. But feet also imply stability and hence firmness—to 'put one's foot down'. Since the foot is the lowest member of the body, in contact with the dust and dirt of the ground, feet are naturally equated with the lowly and humble; so kissing, or washing, the feet of another signifies complete abasement or reverence. When no feet are portayed, as with fire gods, this indicates the instability of flame or fire. In such gods as Ea-Oannes, a fish-body taking the place of feet alludes to the watery element controlled by that deity. Siva, Kali and other divinities treading people underfoot depict the conquering and treading down of worldly passions and the realm of *maya*, the illusory nature of existence. Footprints are either an indication of the path trodden by man, or give evidence of divine presence or visitation. They are then a guide to followers or devotees. Footprints going in opposite directions signify coming and going, past and present, or past and future.

Shoulders are the chief burden-carriers and so are equated with responsibility – to 'take it on one's shoulders'. But to carry a person shoulder-high is to rank him with the gods as not touching the ground but moving through the air.

Kneeling is an attitude of submission, homage to a superior, or supplication, but, on the other hand, knees represent vitality, strength and the generative power and this is the force which is lowered in front of another in the act of kneeling. To place upon the knee is a symbol of adoption, acceptance, a recognition of paternity or of maternal care and responsibility.

The Eye

Either good or evil can come from the eye. Like the pointing finger, the evil eye can be a directive of malefic power and can concentrate energy and ill-will, which, in Celtic mythology, is the direct opposite of the generous heart of compassion. The single eye is also ambivalent. It is evil with the Cyclops or monsters of destructive power, but good as the single eye of enlightenment, of purposefulness, of the self-contained and of eternity. The beneficent eye is associated with omniscience and the all-seeing power of divinity. It is a symbol of all sun gods as the sun is the 'eye of the day', just as the stars are the 'eyes of the night'. These latter also signify omniscience and never-sleeping watchfulness.

The mystic eye is light, knowledge, enlightenment, and the Third Eye of Siva and Buddha is the 'flaming pearl' of transcendent vision, wisdom and spiritual consciousness. The Persian Yima, the Good Shepherd, possesses the solar eye and the secret of immortality. In Egypt the eye symbolism is highly complex. The Eye of Horus, the Utchat, the All-seeing, has been suggested as the Pole Star, as the eye of the mind or illumination. The Eye of Ra is also the Uraeus. The right eye is the sun, Ra and Osiris, and the left eye is the moon and Isis. This is the exact opposite of Chinese and Japanese symbolism in which the left eye is the sun and the right the moon. The Phoenician Cronos has four eyes, two of which are closed and two open in turn, signifying perpetual watchfulness. In Christianity the 'light of the body is in the eye'. The seven eyes of the Apocalypse are the seven Spirits of God. The eye of God is the all-seeing. As has been said, the 'eye of the heart' is spiritual perception, intellectual intuition and illumination. This is of particularly significance in Amerindian symbolism, where 'the eye of the heart sees everything' and is the eye of the Great Spirit. In Islam it represents the spiritual centre, the seat of the Absolute Intellect. This is probably also Plato's meaning when he says 'There is an eye of the soul . . . by it alone is Truth seen.'

The Hair and the Mouth
Another seat of the life-force is the hair, which draws the substance of this power from the head. It is the power of thought and inspiration and, in the male, also represents the physical force, so that cutting the hair, as in a monastic tonsure, or shaving

The Eye of Horus

it off, denotes the ascetic or dedicated religious person renouncing the physical life. Long flowing hair in the female depicts freedom, the virgin, the unmarried. For the married state it used to be bound up, symbolizing the loss of freedom. In Christianity, loose hair also depicts the penitent, as with Mary Magdelene wiping Christ's feet with her unbound hair. As cutting a man's hair shows physical renunciation or loss of power, so cutting a woman's hair deprives her of the power to work magic or cast spells. Tarquin had the hair of Vestal Virgins cut when they married and it was not allowed to grow again. Dishevelled or torn hair is a sign of grief or mourning or of extreme wretchedness; but in Hinduism the matted hair of Siva portrays him as an ascetic, while the black hair of Kali is Time, the Destroyer. When Buddha is depicted with perfectly curled hair it represents control of the life-force, serenity and dispassion. Hair standing on end is not only associated with fear but is a symbol of magic power or of divine possession.

Opening the mouth is synonymous with speech; it is to use the power of speech in uttering 'words of power' and in pronouncing judgement. But mouth symbolism has another aspect; it is also the all-devouring power of the Earth Mother and, again, of Kali as Time. It is, too, equated with the entrance to the underworld, or the belly of the whale, that is death. Death 'swallows' all things. Lips have a share in mouth symbolism, but only as pronouncement. The tongue, however, is more important. It represents preaching, uttering, the voice of the deity. Fleshy tongues are often attributes of demons and monsters in mediaeval Christian art and the Devil is frequently portrayed with a fleshy, protruding tongue. Sumarian monster animals often have extended tongues. But in some places in the East, notably Tibet, putting out the tongue is symbolic of 'out of darkness into light' and can be a form of greeting; it also has an apotropaic significance. It has been suggested that when animals are depicted with tongues hanging out it is a supplication for water from the sky, a plea for rain.

The internal organs of the body are used more in simile and metaphor than in symbolism: being 'liverish', 'as green as bile', 'full of spleen', and so on; but the bowels, which were thought of as the seat of the unrestrained emotions (we speak of this in modern times as 'a gut reaction'), are symbolic of compassion. In Chinese art the intestines can be an interpretation of the mystic knot as compassion and affection on the mundane level and spiritually as the Infinite. In Alchemy, the belly is the laboratory of transformation. In Chinese art the fat belly of the god of wealth, and in Hinduism, of Ganesha, represents gluttony and hence prosperity.

The Womb
The womb naturally signifies the feminine principle, the matrix, the Earth Mother—'the womb of the earth', which gives birth to all things. The cave is its chief symbol; thus, the Dying God of vegetation is born in a cave and emerges from the womb of the earth. The well and all waters and all that encloses or contains, such as walls, caskets and cups, are symbols of the womb. It represents all that is unmanifest, also plenitude and all possibilities. In initiation ceremonies, which often take place in a cave or some enclosed dark space, the symbolism is that of the return to the womb to be born again. Heroes who emerge from their trials having lost their hair, are symbolic of this *regressus ad uterum* and are hairless as a new-born babe. In Alchemy the womb is equated with a mine, the embryo being the ore and the minerals are born of the earth, while man acts as a midwife in aiding nature to hasten the birth.

Sexual Symbolism
The body's function in sex has lost what little myth and symbolism it ever had in the West and so has become a merely physical, and often pathological, preoccupation in a society that is no longer aware of its true meaning and so treats it as a purely physical appetite or an escape mechanism. The prevalence of pornography and a sex-obsessed literature and art is sufficient indication of the sick mind in the sick body, the very opposite of the ideal of *mens sana in corpore sano*. Sex, having been ruthlessly suppressed in Christianity and the West, its symbolism not understood and its myth lost, has become unbalanced and unnatural and has lashed back at its misusers. The more balanced and less inhibited East never allowed body to become divorced from spirit and sex symbolism played its rightful part in both religion and everyday life. In Hinduism the *linga* and *yoni*, the male and female principles, not only represent the functions and union of the two sexes as a physical force, but also reflect cosmic creation, the renewal of life, the active and passive powers of the universe. In Tantric yoga, the two sexes play their part in the union that leads to perfect balance and to the losing of the lower self in the higher Self, the ultimate One. Sex symbolism in these traditions is in no

Male–Female unity

Double triangle:
male–female, fire-water

Serpent depicting
solar–lunar unity

Cross and crescent:
male–female unity

Ionic capital with solar disc
and lunar crescent

way a guise for eroticism since religion is basic and controls everything; bodily union illustrates the soul's union with the divine power.

The perfection of this union is, again, symbolized in the *yin-yang*, which, though its portent goes far beyond sex, is nevertheless, on that level, the best possible expression. Known also as T'ien and Ti, Heaven and Earth, the Two Powers of Nature, they are the great forces at work in the universe; they are absolute balance and unity, bound together in the circle of perfection, forever interacting upon each other. Here, again, the symbolism of 'play' in the creative forces is relevant. Neither power is complete on its own but must, through interplay, produce harmonious unity. The *yin-yang* diagram also depicts the fact that each sex has in itself the germ of the other.

The lost symbolism of the West was earlier embodied in Alchemy, in the *conjunctio*, the union of sulphur and quicksilver, king and queen, gold and silver, sun and moon, which produced the Androgyne and brought mankind back to primordial perfection and wholeness. This is portrayed in the two-faced head of the King-Queen, or in the East by the half-male, half-female figure of the *shakta-shakti*, which also symbolizes the union and interaction of the blind strength of the male and the subtle intuition of the female, of action and reflection, and, indeed, of all the complementary opposites in the universe. Other symbols of union are: the complete circle, two interlocking circles, two interlocking triangles pointing upwards and downwards, trees with intertwining branches, two birds joined with only two wings between them, and, of course all pairs such as king and queen, sun and moon, heaven and earth, and so on.

The Symbolism of Clothes and Ornaments
Clothing, too, is not as symbolic in the West as in the East, where dress and ornaments, particularly those of women, will indicate the estate, whether married or single or widowed, though this applies to some extent to such of the national costumes as still survive in Europe.

Among ornaments, precious stones have an extensive symbolism of their own, such as the diamond representing durability, the sun, light. Its opposite, the pearl, is the feminine principle, the moon and the power of the waters, or, in Chinese symbolism, the *yin* pearl complements the *yang* jade. The green of the emerald is the colour of spring, of youth. The red of the ruby is royalty, dignity, passion, power, while the blue of the sapphire represents the heavens and truth. But to deal with this fully would require a volume in itself.

Usually made of precious metal or precious stones, the necklace, chain or collar are indications of office and dignity, such as the mayor's chain, or in old China, the mandarin's chain; but they also signify the chain that binds the wearer to office and its obligations. A ceremonial belt has the same significance. The links or beads of the chain or necklace represent diversity in unity, the multiplicity of form in the manifest world being held and connected by the thread of unity, the unmanifest. The bracelet is also a symbol of union and of the circle of life. The significance of the ring has already been noted in connection with marriage.

Since the hat covers the head, the seat of the intellectual life-force, it also covers and contains thought, a symbolism which persists in the saying that 'He was wearing a different hat', implying that a different viewpoint or attitude was adopted. Head-covering, from the crown to the cardinal's hat, bishop's mitre, judge's wig, scholar's mortar-board, to the businessman's bowler hat, the top hat and cloth cap, all indicate the lifestyle of the wearer. In earlier times the hat denoted nobility and freedom, in contradistinction to the slave who went bare-headed and bare-footed. The removal of the hat, either raising it in greeting or removing it on entering a sacred place or a house, is a courteous suggestion of inferiority to the person saluted. On crossing a threshold, removing it is part of the ritual threshold symbolism in passing from the outer profane world to the inner sacred one. The same applies to the removal of shoes on entering a temple or mosque.

Like the foot on which it is worn, the shoe can mean movement, hence liberty; but it is also the lowly and humble as it is in contact with dust and dirt, so that it is ritually put off to divest one's self of vice and the unclean. Sandals have a lunar connection, since the moon is the Goddess of the Brazen Sandal which depicts the full moon. Sandals with wings on the heels, as worn by messenger gods, especially Hermes/Mercury, depict fleetness of communication between gods and men.

Just as the extended bare hand is evidence of good faith, so the glove is removed in greeting as a token of both good intention and respect. In the Middle Ages it was also a gauge of honour. To throw it down was to challenge the honour; to pick it up was to accept that challenge.

A cloak is both a sign of dignity and social position; but it is also an ambivalent symbol, being a type of disguise or concealment, thus implying withdrawal, obscurity and the secretive—as in 'cloak and dagger' tactics. The tunic reveals man's true nature, but the cloak hides it. Wizards, witches and magicians wear the cloak to symbolize their mysterious arts and hidden powers of transformation. In Christian art the Devil is often depicted as wearing a black cloak; so do sinister characters in profane art and legend, such as vampires and witches. Queens of Heaven and Sky Gods wear sky-blue mantles.

Ceremonial robes and dresses are, like cloaks and hats, indicative of rank or social occasions, and vestments for religious and ritual functions all have their appropriate significance. Priestly robes have a complex symbolism of their own in all religions. The ceremonial robes of the Chinese Emperors and officials were not only some of the most superb creations of art and craft but presented a symbolism of the entire universe and the power and perfection of Heaven, whose representative on the earth was the Emperor.

Even the ordinary man or woman in the street signals his or her character, preferences and psychological make-up by the clothes chosen and worn and the manner of dress and ornaments adopted. So is mankind surrounded by symbols in everyday contacts and beliefs, each person being, indeed, a living symbol.

Index